MW01493900

Printed by Kindle Enterprise Publishing, Seattle, WA, USA. Available from Amazon.com and other retail outlets.

ISBN: 1724175416   ISBN-13: 978-1724175410

Mention of specific companies, organizations, or authorities in this book does not imply endorsement by the author or publisher, nor does mention of specific companies, organizations, or authorities imply that they endorse this book, its author, or the publisher.

2 4 6 8 10 9 7 5 3 1   20 19 18

Book design, garment construction, content, and illustrations by Kaitlyn Dornbier
Contributing photographers: Brooke Davis, Sara Mulders, and Avery Stahr

NOT YOUR GRANDMA'S
sewing guide

KAITLYN DORNBIER

In loving memory,
"Get your shit together and get it together now."
- Grandma Melva June Pals

table of contents

let's fucking do this

Start a new fucking hobby. Do something with your hands other than scroll on your fucking phone screen. Start a project, leave it half-done for a month, and come back to it. Get excited about something - really, truly excited. Daydream on the bus and in the grocery line. Pin something online and think to yourself, 'I could make that,' and then

actually fucking follow through.

Spend your last $16 on some fabric because your heart and your head and your hands want it. Stay up until 2:00am making a stupid pair of pajama bottoms. Be overly proud of your first sweatshirt, with its shitty seams and uneven hem, because you pulled its entire existence out of the ether and made it tangible. Spend a whole Netflix season sewing one skirt. Have some 'me' time. Make something for yourself or your grandma or your dog. Shrug your shoulders and say 'that's good enough'. Grit your teeth and make a third fucking trip to the craft store. Care and try and be frustrated. Just start something fucking new.

This guide is for anyone who doesn't know what the fuck they're doing with a sewing machine, but would sort of like to.

It's for the people who had home-ec class in high school but don't remember shit, and for people who never had the opportunity to learn. It's for anyone whose grandma was a great seamstress, everyone whose mothers can't sew a straight line, and those gents who'd rather sit down at a sewing machine than at a video game console - you do you.

Sewing is a useful-as-fuck, forgotten skill. If you mention to someone that you sew, the first thing out of their mouth is, "That's so neat, it's such a lost art," followed by, "So, like, could you alter a pair of pants for me?" Let's take a second to digest that - by mentioning one fucking fact,

you are now uniquely talented and in high demand.

Yes, sewing is a dwindling hobby, but why bother going to a fabric store, measuring, cutting, and stitching it all together when you can drop $4.99 at a Forever 21 and call it a fucking day? Because learning a new skill is bigger than one top. It's making kick-ass Halloween costumes for your kids someday, and salvaging your favorite way-too-worn-out leggings with the hole in them and the wine stain, and earning a little beer money hemming jeans for the frat boys down the hall. You're already unique and talented and in high demand, give yourself a hobby that emphasizes that.

This guide was put together for the beginner of beginners - for those lazy sons of bitches, like me, who want to learn the basics as well as what you can basically skip over. The examples aren't perfection, but your first trials wont be, either - this is a safe, messy, perfectly imperfect space. The first section lays out what to look for in a new sewing machine, what must-have tools to throw in your Amazon shopping cart, and how to navigate the fabric aisles for the first time. The second section covers the ins and outs of using your machine; the stitches, seams, and hems to set your ass on the path to

greatness, as well as quick fixes for when shit starts to go south. The pièce de résistance, the third section, is the foundation for sewing actual fucking garments. Working with patterns, making your own super-duper novice patterns, and the no-frills steps for sewing all of the closet staples. This section will be your bible to the fashion fundamentals, hand to God and Coco Chanel. The last section explains the extra elements to elevate your shit to the next level. Pockets, buttons, zippers - all of the little things that you don't really need, but you really do need, you know? In the spirit of putting-in-as-little-effort-as-possible, I've including a quick and dirty diagram of alterations, and a fabric-buying chart to save time and money at the store.

Let's be realistic - you aren't going to learn every sewing trick in a weekend. Hell, you might take a month to sew a descent straight line. Start with simple, bare-bones projects, and work your way to the bells and whistles. This guide was (hopefully) set up to help you do just that. The fundamental projects are explained in the most cut, stitch, and call-it-quits way possible, with helpful tricks thrown in and where/when/how to cut corners.

In fashion, there are a gajilliion different variations of one simple top. To have an illustrated tutorial of every single garment you could make (as a beginner alone!) would be fucking lunacy. Instead, the guide will list detour page numbers where they might be relevant - 'If you want to add pockets to your skirt, check out page 68'. It's not that damned difficult, but is another reason to start simple and have a plan beforehand. If you learn one stupid lesson from this entire book, it's have a motherfucking plan. One more time; Have. A. Mother. Fucking. Plan. Difficulty levels should help gauge when you're in way over your head, but nothing is so hecking hard you couldn't figure it out with a little poking around.

You're creative, you're capable, and you're so ready for whatever-the-fuck magic you're about to make.

want to skip the bullshit?

Already familiar with how to make a simple stitch on that sexy sewing machine of yours? Just have no attention span and want to get after this in that fly-by-the-seam-of-your-pants way? We've all been there - I, too, throw away the cake mix box and dig it back out of the trash a few times before my cake is baked. Skip ahead to these sections to fast-track this delightful journey:

Find the easiest fabrics to work with on page 9

Get the gist of using or making a pattern on page 34

Begin assembling basics garments on page 44

Let Me Be Your Guide

Look for the following symbols throughout the book for useful-as-fuck tips and corners to cut to make this as painless as possible:

 Directions to pages you might jump to next

  Tried-and-true hacks you should definitely utilize

  Shit you can skip if you're feeling lazy

  Difficulty levels to gauge how many fucks you'll need

shit to get started

Tools of the Trade

Welcome to your new, fucking fabulous hobby. Those embarking on a brand new hobby can be divided into two groups when it comes to buying tools and supplies; My Mother and Me. If you are like My Mother, you've already bought every tool imaginable and two other beginners manuals besides this one. Congratulations, you are covered. If you are more like Me, you'll buy, beg, or borrow the bare necessities and make do for the rest. There's a list of the essentials to save yourself headache and heartbreak later on in your projects, as well as tips for picking out fabric for the first time. The goal here is to minimize hassle and not max out your credit card.

New to your sewing machine? The important parts are pointed out in a handy diagram, and hopefully the explanations of the extra pieces will get you on the right track to, you know, start sewing some shit.

Your Machine

Your sewing machine is the most important tool - sur-fucking-prise! - when you're planning to sew something. (We could get into the dirty details of hand-sewing but no one's got time for that shit). If you're shopping for a new sewing machine, the sheer amount of options can be daunting - huge price differences, features out the ass, and ever-newer and crazier computerized gizmos that make this whole thing look a lot more complicated than it is. I'm including some helpful hints on what to look for in a beginner machine so you don't feel like such an idiot in the store.

You don't need the biggest and best to be able to make something fabulous, but you do need something that suits your needs. Salespeople in fabric stores are some of the best people on earth - let them know you're a beginner and ask to try out or see some of the machines in action - these mini demonstrations can be great jumping-off lessons. Keep in mind that bigger and more complicated does not always mean better, and your clothes won't suffer because you *gasp* had to turn the knob by hand instead of selecting a stitch on a screen - 'tis a poor carpenter who blames his tools.

Whatever the mechanism, some machines come with at least a handful of built-in stitches and you'll want to look for something that, at the very least, can do a basic straight stitch and a zig-zag stitch. If you think you might try tackling athletic clothing, look for some double-or-triple stitches as well - they hold stretchy fabric together better when you're downward-dogging. Some other useful features I swear up and down by are the instant-reverse button (not for 'un-sewing', but for backstitching to secure shit), a thread-cutter near the needle, and a built-in buttonholer. With these, my friends, you will conquer the world.

The diagram shows the basic parts of a sewing machine, with some explanations to what the fuck they do. Your machine will be different, and I cannot stress enough how helpful your machines manual will be - you will drag it out every time you need to change the needle, you will spill coffee on it and crumple the cover, and you will know by heart that the twin needle instructions are on page 62. Most even include helpful hints in the back as to what-the-fuck-is-that-sound and why-the-fuck-won't-you-start, so take heed and read your god damn manual.

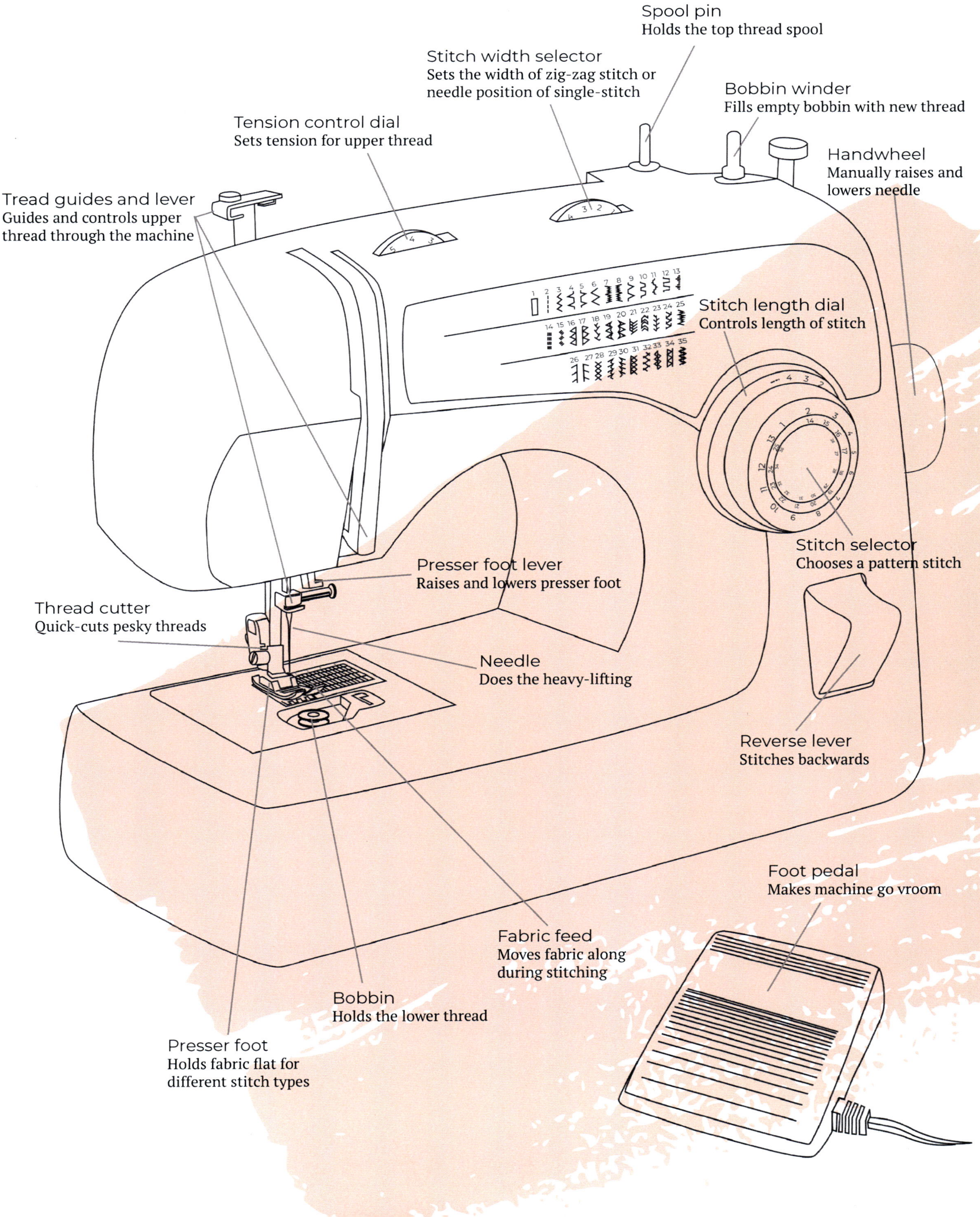

Spool pin
Holds the top thread spool

Stitch width selector
Sets the width of zig-zag stitch or
needle position of single-stitch

Bobbin winder
Fills empty bobbin with new thread

Handwheel
Manually raises and
lowers needle

Tension control dial
Sets tension for upper thread

Tread guides and lever
Guides and controls upper
thread through the machine

Stitch length dial
Controls length of stitch

Stitch selector
Chooses a pattern stitch

Presser foot lever
Raises and lowers presser foot

Thread cutter
Quick-cuts pesky threads

Needle
Does the heavy-lifting

Reverse lever
Stitches backwards

Foot pedal
Makes machine go vroom

Fabric feed
Moves fabric along
during stitching

Bobbin
Holds the lower thread

Presser foot
Holds fabric flat for
different stitch types

Machine Accessories

Needles

The type of needle you use may change depending on the fabric and stitch type. Ninety-nine percent of the time, beginners will make the use of a universal needle. A ballpoint needle can tag in for stretchier knits, but the real unsung hero is the twin needle - used to sew two rows of stitches at once, it is endlessly useful for stretchy hems and athletic wear. You will need to replace your needles every so often, especially when your machine starts skipping stitches or stopping up mid-seam. If you're using a hand-me-down machine, it may be a good idea to replace the needle right away and save yourself some what-the-fucks early on.

Bobbins

Bobbins are mini spools that hold what will be the 'bottom' thread in your machine, and they will either be removable or built-in for winding. Always start with an empty bobbin, and don't wind it too full. Snip any excess thread from the top after spooling as it can get caught up and wreak unsuspecting havoc on your project.

Feet

If your machine comes with extra accessory feet, give a cheer! Your life just became way more interesting. More helpful feet include a zipper foot (for attaching zippers, fucking duh), a buttonhole foot (again, duh), a walking foot for fabrics that are finicky to feed through the machine (think leather or super-stretchy knits), a narrow hemmer foot for the teensy hems on thin fabrics, and a blind stitch foot for making magical invisible hems. Again, consult The Manual for exactly how to use the different attachments.

Read your motherfucking manual.

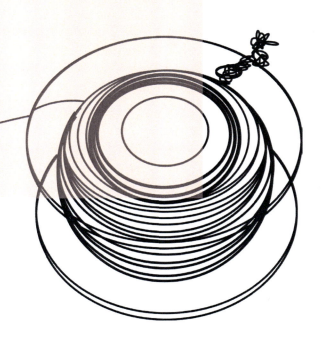

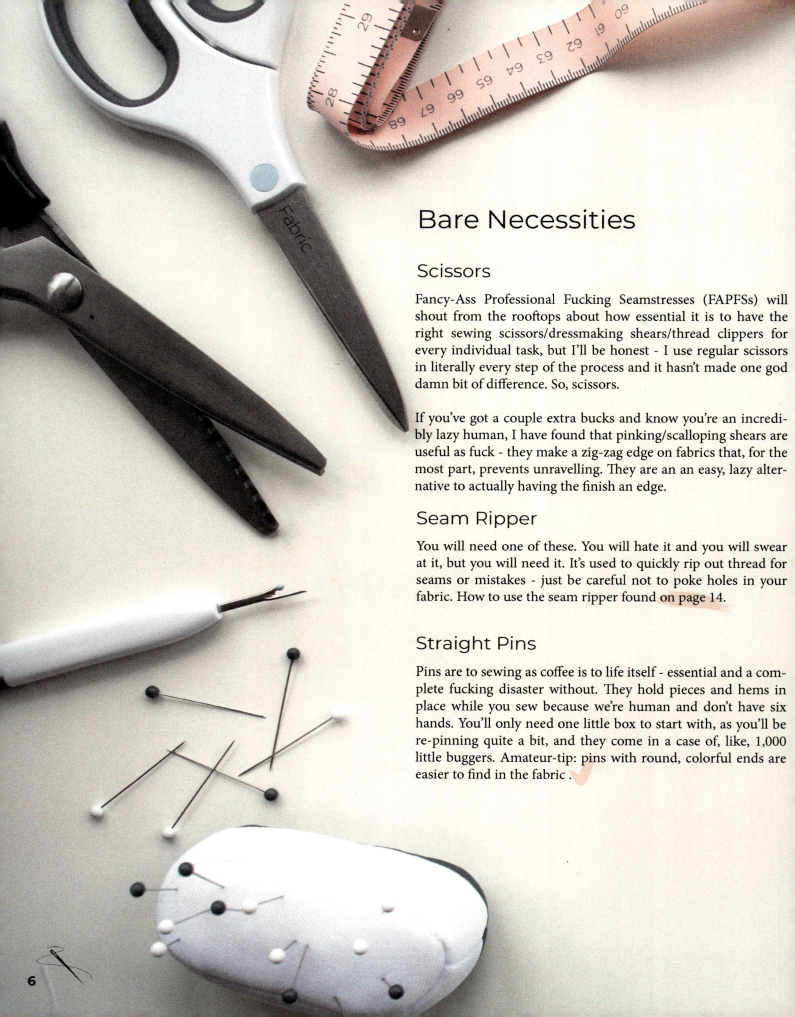

Bare Necessities

Scissors

Fancy-Ass Professional Fucking Seamstresses (FAPFSs) will shout from the rooftops about how essential it is to have the right sewing scissors/dressmaking shears/thread clippers for every individual task, but I'll be honest - I use regular scissors in literally every step of the process and it hasn't made one god damn bit of difference. So, scissors.

If you've got a couple extra bucks and know you're an incredibly lazy human, I have found that pinking/scalloping shears are useful as fuck - they make a zig-zag edge on fabrics that, for the most part, prevents unravelling. They are an an easy, lazy alternative to actually having the finish an edge.

Seam Ripper

You will need one of these. You will hate it and you will swear at it, but you will need it. It's used to quickly rip out thread for seams or mistakes - just be careful not to poke holes in your fabric. How to use the seam ripper found on page 14.

Straight Pins

Pins are to sewing as coffee is to life itself - essential and a complete fucking disaster without. They hold pieces and hems in place while you sew because we're human and don't have six hands. You'll only need one little box to start with, as you'll be re-pinning quite a bit, and they come in a case of, like, 1,000 little buggers. Amateur-tip: pins with round, colorful ends are easier to find in the fabric .

Ruler

How much you use your tape measure will depend on how precise you're trying to be when making a garment. You'll need it to find your body measurements, but also to measure sleeve holes, make edges line up, and place darts.

While a tape measure can certainly do the job, a seam gauge (not shown) is helpful if you're feeling very extra. It's a small ruler with a sliding bit that helps keep your hems, pleats, and buttonholes even.

Marking Tools

FAPFSs will tell you every damned type of fabric needs its own marking tool. Marking tools are needed to transfer pattern markings onto fabric, or to label which pattern piece is which, but, as long as you're only marking on the wrong side of the fabric, any old pencil or pen will do. I picked up a white fabric pencil to use on darker fabrics because you can never have too many little black dresses (read: I have too many little black dresses). Note, tailors chalk and fabric pencils are not the same thing - tailors chalk rubs off super easily and thus seems pointless to me.

Thread

Like needles, thread comes in a blessed, all-purpose universal thread that you will use for most of your beginner projects. Technically, you should match the thread you choose to the weight of the fabric and size of your needle, like using extra-fine thread for lightweight fabrics or heavy thread for jeans, but - technically - we don't give a fuck for right now. Universal, it is - just opt for a thread color that matches or compliments your project fabric.

Iron and Ironing Board

Pressing is done by gently using an iron along seams or hems to make helpful, deliberate cres in the fabric. As annoying as it is, pressing is the one step in sewing a garment that FAPFSs will harp on to their dying breath. They say it saves time in the long run (I'm sure it does, and I'm just fucking lazy), but mostly it makes shit look more official. If you don't already own them, go out and pick up an iron and small ironing board because we're god damn adults and you should have them anyways.

If you plan on using super lightweight fabric or interfacing, you'll also want to grab a press cloth (or make one yourself from a lightweight fabric) - it protects from iron shine and is needed for fusible interfacing.

Picking Fabric

Choosing what fabric to use for a project is a fucking minefield. Patterns give suggestions for what fabrics work best and stores try their damndest to organize your options into helpful categories, but it isn't always so cut-and-DIY. Again, fabric store salespeople? Sent from heaven. If you're really lost, asking for help is the quickest way to just get the hell out of there and onto sewing. If you are making up a pattern or don't like the choices in the 'suggested fabrics', explore the whole store. The first little black dress I made used men's suit material because it had the fabric feel I was looking for (referred to in professional circles as the hand of the fabric), so I'm including a mental checklist of what to take into account when wandering the wovens.

Weight — The weight of a fabric can refer to many things, but for now we'll use it to gauge sheerness and decide if you'll need to add lining to your design. Help with picking lining fabric on page 84.

Softness — Softness is next to godliness - in most cases. There's a dick joke in here somewhere, but we've not the time. Fabrics that are too soft wont hold their shape, and rough fabrics will need a soft layer of lining to make them comfortable.

Stretchiness — Fabrics will either stretch in one direction or two. Clothing fits most comfortably when the fabric is stretchiest horizontally (across the chest, shoulders, hips, etc). Your pattern layout will depend on which direction the fabric stretches.

Drape — If you hang a layer of the fabric over your arm, you'll notice the drape of the fabric - if it falls loose or holds its shape. Knowing what sort of drape you're looking for takes practice, so go with your gut.

Easiest to Start With

If you're using a pattern, it should give a list of compatible fabric types. Sans pattern, medium-weight knits or plain weaves are great for beginners because they go through the machine easily, dramatically reducing the amount of 'fucks' muttered to yourself at 2:00 am. These fabrics also won't unravel at the edges, meaning you can save some sanity and thread and skip seam-finishing. Knits with descent stretch offer wiggle-room (literally) with your projects, and picking solid-color or all-over-pattern fabric makes laying out a pattern easier. Hide stitching imperfections on beginner projects by choosing softer materials like cotton, matching your thread as closely as possible with the main fabric color, or opting for small, dark prints that don't need to be perfectly matched up at the edges (think overall prints or smaller stripes).

Avoid super lightweight, sheer fabrics to start with, as they're tricky to feed through the machine and need perfect, delicate seam finishes and hems to look anything other than shitty.

Fabric Information

Fabric will normally be stocked in bolts on shelves around the store. The bolts will have labels on the end that list the price per yard, the width of the fabric, care instructions, and fiber percentages. Fiber percentages are helpful for knowing how stretchy something will be (depending on percentage of spandex) or if you should pre-wash your fabric before cutting a pattern (like with 100% cotton). Basically, a lot of helpful shit. Snapping a picture of it on your phone is quick, easy, and surprisingly useful later on.

How Much to Buy

Do you know that Math Lady meme with all of the number equations orbiting her poor, confused face? That will be you, standing in the aisle, trying to calculate how much goddamn fabric to buy for a project. It's tricky, so I'm including a table on page 90 to save you a xanax and an extra trip to the store. If you choose a fabric with a 'right way' pattern, plaids, or napped fabrics like velvet, you'll need to buy ¼ yard extra for each yard needed, so all pieces can be cut facing the same direction.

To those extra-organized bitches (talking to you, girl with a bullet journal and labeled pantry containers), make note of how much fabric you buy for a project and refer to it for later, similar projects.

using your motherfucking machine

Seams and Shit

Saddle up, ladies and gentlemen, you're about to make that sewing machine your bitch. What the hell is a seam? How's that different from a damn hem? Why do my stitches look shitty? All these questions and more will be answered in this section. From basic stitches to bitchin' stitches, with some tips along the way about dealing with machine trouble, navigating stitch lines, and a dizzying amount of different sewing variations to tackle almost any project.

You don't have to master every option in this section before you start your first project - ain't nobody got time for that. You can do a helluva lot with just one straight stitch, and might go months without wondering what the hell else your machine can do. Get comfortable making a basic seam, and come back to explore the other crap as you get the hang of it. After a little practice on some scrap fabric, you can ride off into the fucking sunset.

The Basics

The two most basic stitches are straight and zig-zag. By changing the stitch length and width dials, you can vary the size and placement of the stitch line.

The diagram below shows the different stitch length and width combinations for straight and zig-zag stitches. It's not too fucking complicated - just note that the straight stitch 'width' is how far to the left the stitch line will be made.

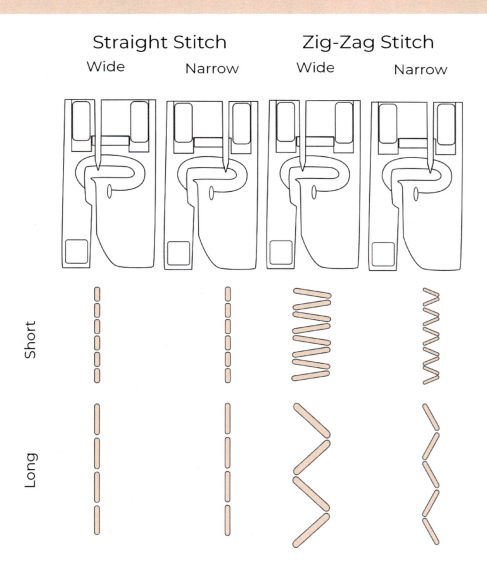

Straight Stitch		Zig-Zag Stitch	
Wide	Narrow	Wide	Narrow

Short

Long

Winding a Bobbin

Follow your motherfucking machine guide for bobbin-winding instructions, but with these helpful tips:

✓ Always start with an empty bobbin

✓ Don't wind that shit too full

✓ The little extra dangler should be cut off after winding

Tensions

Tensions are tricky - I won't lie to you. Basically, you want the top thread tension and the bottom thread tension to be equal, but you have to do a little work to get there. Too tight, and the fabric puckers or your thread breaks. Too little tension, and your stitch is weak and loose.

Always adjust tension on a piece of scrap fabric before diving into the real thing. The lighter the fabric, the lower your tension will probably be. Make sure to only change tension with the pressure foot raised so the new tension 'catches'. If you're brand fucking new, use different color top thread and bobbin thread to more easily spot the adjustments.

Correct   Stitches meet in the middle and lie flat, no fabric puckering.

Too Tight   Stitch links are pulled to the top of the fabric, and the thread may break while sewing. Fabric might pucker. Dial that fucker down.

Too Loose   Stitch links are pulled to the bottom layer of fabric, and the stitches look loose. Some stitches are skipped and the fabric may get pulled down into the machine.

Too Loose

Too Tight

Correct

'Good Enough' or 'Gotta Redo It'?

It's the last seam on The Project That Will Never Fucking End. Or the third time you've tried to put that motherfucking zipper in. Or you've made the seam on the wrong goddamn side of the fabric. Whatever the issue, you will grapple with yourself, "Should I redo it?". Let me help you out.

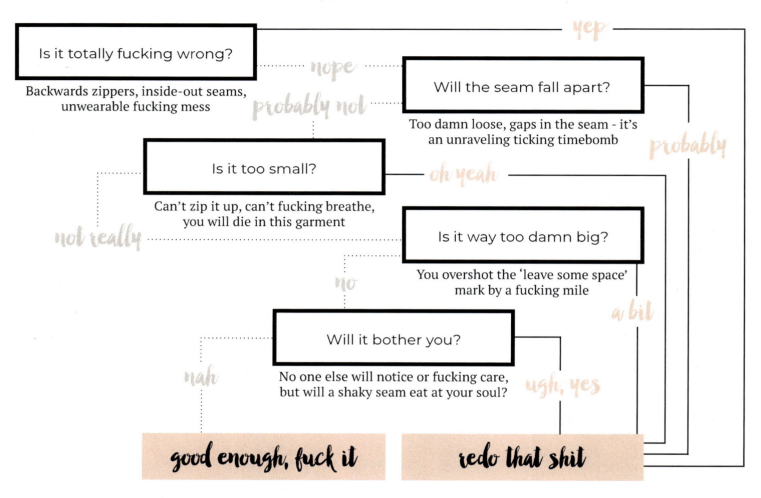

Is it totally fucking wrong?
Backwards zippers, inside-out seams, unwearable fucking mess

yep

nope

probably not

Will the seam fall apart?
Too damn loose, gaps in the seam - it's an unraveling ticking timebomb

probably

Is it too small?
Can't zip it up, can't fucking breathe, you will die in this garment

oh yeah

not really

Is it way too damn big?
You overshot the 'leave some space' mark by a fucking mile

no

a bit

Will it bother you?
No one else will notice or fucking care, but will a shaky seam eat at your soul?

nah

ugh, yes

good enough, fuck it

redo that shit

Ripping Out Shitty Stitches

You're going to fuck up, and when you do, your trusty seam ripper will be there to save your ass. Ripping out stitches can be done two ways.

Pull the two fabric pieces taut to see the seam ravine, and pick out the stitches one or two at a time - don't slide that shit along the seam or you'll end up putting a hole in the fabric.

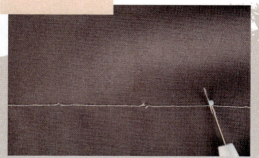

On one side of the fabric, cut every few stitches. You may need to cut more stitches on this side if the seam is very tight.

Flip the fabric over and pull up the thread. Pick the rest of the top thread out easily with your fingers or tape.

Most Common Machine Problems (and Fixes)

No machine is perfect, and it will take you a while to instinctively troubleshoot what the hell is going wrong. You will tackle all of these problems at least once in your sewing experience. If you run into an issue, stop, take a sip/glass/bottle of wine, and fix it. Most of the time, you won't need to rip out the whole seam you were just working on, just restart about an inch back on top of your last good stitches.

The top thread keeps slipping out of the stupid needle before sewing.
Make sure the upper thread guide is at the top before you start sewing, so it doesn't pull up and out when you press the pedal. Also, hold the thread ends out behind the foot with your left hand when beginning to sew.

The goddamn fabric is slipping around.
Put the fucking presser foot down.

The fabric isn't moving along.
Is the presser foot down? If the fabric is too stretchy, you may need to change the tension or switch to a fancy-ass 'walking foot'. You can gently pull the fabric along through the machine while you sew. Lengthening the stitch could also help.

Thread is bunching or 'bird-nesting' on the underside of the fabric.
This problem is annoying as hell and often goes unnoticed until you're done making a seam. Work the piece back and forth gently to loosen the piece from the machine without putting a hole in the fabric. Make sure to get all the extra thread out from inside the machine, and then take the whole seam out with your seam ripper. Rethread the top and bottom with the presser foot raised, and then check the tension on a scrap piece.

Fabric is being pulled down into the mother-fucking machine.
If the fabric is too stretchy, you'll need to gently stretch the fabric more taut and pull it along. If the problem happens repeatedly, your needle is too dull or not the right type and should be replaced. If neither is the problem, your tension is wildly off.

Your machine keeps halting.
Is the needle hitting the foot? You'll need to re-attach the foot and replace the needle that's probably bent, broken, or dull. Do a few hand-cranked stitches slowly to make sure the stitch width is right for whatever foot you're using.

Check if the bobbin thread got wound around the bobbin. This happens if the bobbin thread has gotten loose or is nearing empty. You'll need to cut the bobbin thread, unwind the bobbin to a good, tight starting point or completely rewind the bobbin anew, and rethread the bottom. If you cut out the bunched up underside-thread you can start sewing again on top of your last good stitches.

The top thread tension may just be too high, try loosening it a bit.

If all else fails, your needle is too dull (or bent) or your fabric is just too thick. Replace your needle with a sharp son-of-a-bitch and sew on.

Your goddamn needle broke.
These may be the most 'What the fuck?!' moments in sewing. Is the stitch width on the right setting for the foot you're using? Whenever you change a foot, slowly lower the needle by hand a few times to make sure the needle wont jam into the foot.
Is your stitch type on the right setting for the foot you're using? For example, narrow hemmer feet often require a straight stitch, not a zig-zag.

Was your needle fully and securely installed? When needles are swapped out, you've really got to shove that fucker up there and tighten it down. Wiggle a newly-replaced needle a little to reassure yourself.

Seams

A 'seam' is considered anywhere two pieces of fabric are sewn together, and is usually made on the 'wrong' side of the fabric. This is different from a 'hem' (page 26), like the bottom of a shirt or sleeve where the edge is just finished. Seems easy (pun intended), but some of you are goddamn beginners and I've got your back.

Sewing a Plain Seam

The beginner's guide to beginning - let's begin. Sewing a straight seam is somehow both easier than expected, and harder. Go slowly, let the machine do the work, and accept that it won't be perfect at first.

Pin that shit right sides together along the whole seam length. The 'right side' of the fabric is whatever side you want to face 'outward' when you wear it. Some fabric looks the same on both sides, so just pick one side and go with it.

Most of the fabric should be to the left of the machine needle, and it will be pulled away from you as you sew. Guide your fabric through gently, careful not to let your right hand get pulverized.

Backstitch at the beginning to keep the stitches from coming undone at this end of the seam. Take a peak at the backstitch instructions below.

WTF is Backstitching?

'Backstitching' is making a few stitches back and forth to lock that seam down. To backstitch at the beginning of a seam, start about an inch into the fabric and sew in reverse almost to the edge of the fabric. Then, stitch forward on top of the line of reversed stitches and keep sewing like normal. At the end of a seam, stitch almost to the edge of the fabric and then make a line of reverse stitches on top of your seam to secure that shit.

There are three main parts of a seam that are referenced regularly; the seam itself, the seam allowance, and the finish. The 'seam' is the actual line of stitches that holds the two pieces of fabric together. You'll use a regular straight stitch most of the time, but the next page shows some different stitch variations useful for stretchy fabric and shit. The 'seam allowance' is the space between the stitched seam and the cut edge. The 'finish' of a seam is what you do to the cut edge, explained more on page 19.

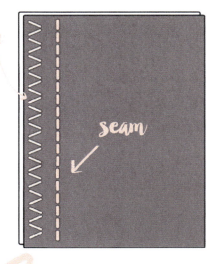

finish

seam

seam allowance

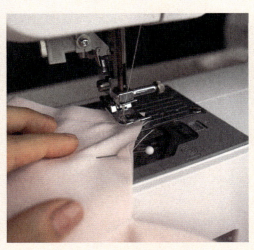

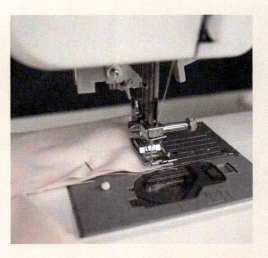

Take the pins out as you sew, slowing or stopping before the pin reaches the foot. Don't be afraid to stop your machine - just try to do it when the needle is down in the fabric so you don't accidentally pull the fabric askew.

At any point where the seam needs to pivot, stop the machine with the needle in the fabric, lift the presser foot, adjust the fabric, and continue sewing straight. Easy-fucking-peasy.

At the end of a seam, backstitch again. Lift the presser foot, pull the piece away from the needle, and cut the top and bottom thread. Trim any excess thread from, and you've made a motherfucking seam!

FAPFSs will tell you to press/iron your seams flat and open after you make them. Does it look nice? Sure. Is it necessary? Hell no. Go with your gut on whether or not you want to press your seams.

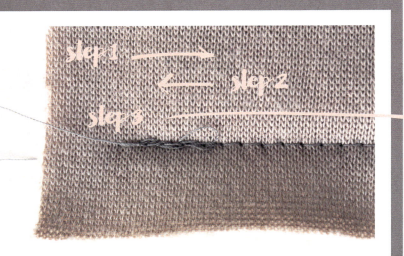

step 1
step 2
step 3

Seam Stitches

Single Stitch
The single stitch is your best fucking friend - you will use it the most often and with most types of fabrics. The only thing the single stitch isn't handy for is stretchy fabrics. Finish the single stitch with one of the edge finishes on the next couple pages.

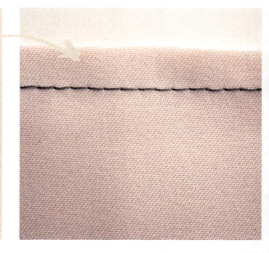

All basic seam stitches are easy as hell.

Double or Tripple Stitch
I couldn't live without the motherfucking tripple-stitch. If your machine has a double- or tripple-stitch built in, you can sew your fabric like normal and still keep elasticity. Since most stretchy fabric doesn't need edge finishing, you can trim the excess fabric and call it a day.

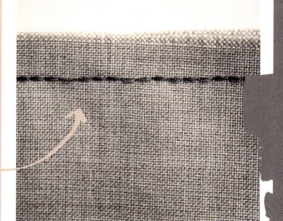

Zigzag and Straight Stitch
To make a seam and finish the edge at the same time, go for the straight-and-zig-zag-duo. Many machines will have this stitch as an all-in-one option, and it's fucking fantastic for knits. If the stitch isn't built in, you can mimic it by sewing a line of straight stitches (stretching gently as you sew), and then going back and sewing a line of zig-zag in the seam allowance. Trim any excess fabric close up to the zig-zag stitch.

Extra Single Stitch
If you don't have a zig-zag stitch, or are worried about strain, adding a second line of straight stitch in the seam allowance will add some strength. Gently stretch the fabric as you sew to preserve some elasticity, and trim the fabric as close to the second row of stitches to finish.

I-Barely-Give-A-Shit Seam Finishes

'Finishing a seam' means 'what do I do with the ugly-ass raw edge?'. Pros: finishing a seam keeps fabric from unraveling, helps a garment last longer through wearing and washing, and looks nicer. Cons: the extra steps are annoying as all-get-out to Team Lazy. The type of seam finish you choose depends on your fabric and the amount of fucks you give.

All finishing examples start with a regular straight-stitch seam, and are no-brainers.

Straight and Pinked

Make a line of straight stitches in the seam allowance, and then trim the excess with pinking shears. This is for-fucking-sure the easiest finish.

Zig-Zag and Cut

If you don't have pinking shears, zig-zag stitch in the seam allowance, and trim the excess with regular scissors.

Miscellaneous Stitch

Some of the other stitches on your machine can add a stronger, better-looking finish, like the zig-zag-and-straight duo. Test a few out on scrap fabric and trim the excess.

Up-Your-Game Seam Finishes

Once you've made the easy seam finishes your bitch, take a peak at more interesting options.

 Bias-Bound

I can't imagine using this one for anything but the inside of a thick jacket.

Step 1 You'll need to buy or make a strip of bias tape (page 29), which just seems like a lot of extra work.

Step 2 Fold the bias tape around the cut edge, with the thicker side underneath, and stitch the whole thing closed.

 Turned and Stitched

Good for most fabrics, but tough to turn over and pin on delicate shit.

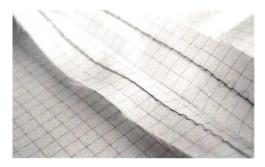

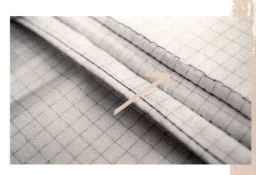

Step 1 (Optionally) make a line of straight stitches in the seam allowance, leaving space to fold over.

Step 2 Turn the seam allowance under - the straight stitches from the first step help with fussy fabrics.

Step 3 Make a line of straight stitches close to the edge, holding the fold in place. Only sew into the seam allowance, don't sew the main fabric of the garment.

 Self-Bound

Best with lighter fabric, as the seam will be bulkier, and for sheer shit because the raw edge is hidden.

Step 1 Trim one side of the seam allowance down close to the stitch line.

Step 2 Fold over the other side of the seam allowance (twice) so no raw edges are visible.

Step 3 Make a straight stitch on the folded edge, preferably close to the original stitches, holding the fold down.

French Seam

This finish is fan-fucking-tastic, but I wouldn't suggest using it anywhere with a curve or turn in the seam - in fact, maybe just use it on side seams.

Step 1 Make your first seam with the *wrong sides* of the fabric together. So, opposite of what you usually do. Trim the excess down.

Step 2 Flip the garment over (so the right sides of the fabric are together) and pin the edge as flat as possible, sandwiching around the seam allowance.

Step 3 Stitch far enough from the edge that the excess you trimmed down in step one is completely encased.

Fake French Seam

Equally as handy as the french finish, but can be done when you've messed up and forgotten to make your first seam with the wrong sides of the fabric together.

Step 1 Make your seam with enough seam allowance that it's easy to fold over.

Step 2 Fold both seam allowances inward - this can be tricky with very delicate or very thick fabrics.

Step 3 Stitch close to the fold to make sure both sides are caught.

Hong Kong Finish

Similar to bias-bound, I don't know when you'd use this bizarre finish, but at least you have it. This will also require either buying or making bias tape (page 29). It's also a pain to explain, so bear with me.

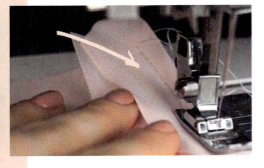

Step 1 Ling up your bias tape and seam allowance on the right edge. Stitch the bias tape to the seam allowance, and trim the edge down.

Step 2 Fold the bias tape over the edge. You can fold the cut edge under again, or leave it free on the underside.

Step 3 Stitch the bias tape fold closed, as close to the 'ditch' as possible. The ditch is the place where the bias tape meets the fabric.

Top-Stitch Seam Finishes

Athletic clothes are all about top-stitch seam finishes, because they hold the seam allowances flat, add durability, and look all...sporty and shit.

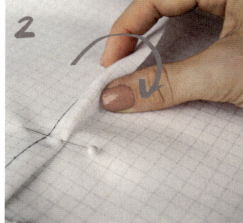

Flat-Fell Seam

Step 1
Make your first seam with the *wrong sides* of the fabric together. Then, trim one side of the seam allowance.

Step 2
Fold the longer seam allowance under and pin so that all cut edges are hidden.

Step 3
Stitch the fold down, as close to the edge of the fold as you can.

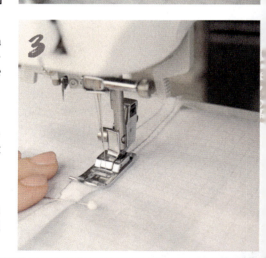

Final
The bottom side will show just a line of stitches where the fold is held down, but the top side will show both the original seam and the stitch holding the fold down.

Fake Flat-Fell Seam

Step 1 Trim one side of the seam allowance down, and press them both to that side - longer seam allowance covering up the shorter.

Step 2 From the right side of the fabric, straight-stitch down through both the top fabric and the seam allowance.

Step 3 Make a second line of top-stitching close to the original seam line. This is purely for decorative effect. Extra-as-fuck.

Final The bottom side will show the original seam, the stitch line holding the seam allowance down, and the extra decorative seam close to the original seam. The top will show the two decorative seams.

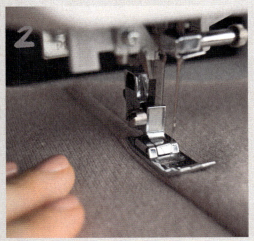

Welt Seam

Step 1
Trim one side of the seam allowance down, and press them both to that side - longer seam allowance covering up the shorter.

Step 2
From the right side, straight-stitch down through both the top fabric and the seam allowance.

Final
The bottom side will show two lines of stitching - the original seam and the stitch holding the longer seam allowance down. The top side will just have the one line of decorative stitching where the seam allowance is held down.

23

Curved Seams

Curved seams may be few and far between when you first start sewing - they're found in fitted bodices and shit (not to be mistaken with armholes, collars, or circle skirt hems - those are 'technically' straight seams that just happen to come back around). When you sew on a curve, use shorter stitch lengths and slow it down.

Step 1 A staystitch (next page) on both sides of a curved hem isn't the worst idea in the world. Make clips into the seam allowance here instead of in Step 3 to make pinning easier.

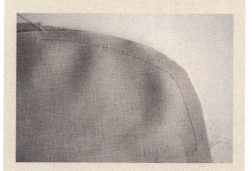

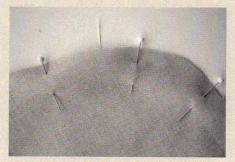

Step 2 Pining curved seams can be a bitch if the fabric wants to pucker or cave. Line up the pieces correctly with more pins, closer together.

Step 3 Notches or slits cut into the seam allowance will let the fabric lay flatter when it's actually worn. Careful not to cut the seam stitch.

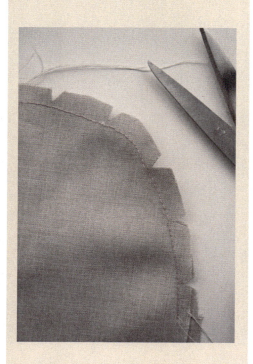

Note: If you make your slits in Step 1 instead of Step 3, it's alright that the notches don't line up when you pin and sew.

Other Useful as Hell Stitches

Here are some other handy stitches to keep in your back pocket.

Understitch

Understitching is goddamn difficult to explain or show in pictures. To keep collar facing (page 65) from flipping up and out, you stitch the facing and seam allowances together. Most of the time it's easiest to stitch with the facing on top and seam allowances underneath, feeling for the seam allowances underneath with your right hand as you go.

Topstitch

Topstitching is any time you sew directly onto the right side of the fabric (aka the outside of the garment faces upwards when you're using your machine). Sometimes it's purely decoration, sometimes it's because you just need to see what the fuck you're doing from the right side.

Bastestitch

The bastestitch is a badass - it's used as a temporary stitch, like when you're trying to test how something will fit. Some machines will have an actual basting stitch option, otherwise just use a straight stitch set to the longest length and loosen your tension a shit-ton. Remove any visible bastestitch after you've finished your actual seams.

Reinforcement Stitch

Reinforcement stitching is smart to put anywhere that may see a lot of tension - the 'v' of a v-neck, armpit areas, etc, or anywhere that will be clipped into. Throw an extra line of straight stitching in the seam allowance to secure it.

Gather Stitch

More gathering details on page 80, but to make it short and sweet - if you sew a line of long, super loose straight stitches, and then tug on the bottom thread, your fabric will gather up nicely.

Staystitch

A staystitch is just a regular straight stitch made close to the cut edge to keep your fabric from stretching out while you're getting your shit together. You'd mostly use it somewhere with a curve or an angle (think necklines or circle-skirt waistlines).

Hems and Finishes

A 'hem' is the bottom of a top, dress, or pants while a 'finish' is any other place on a garment where the cut edge is made to look descent - like sleeveless top armholes. (Confusingly named the same as a 'seam finish', who-the-fuck knows why).

Hemming will always happen last, so, per Murphy's Law, it's also when you're most likely to run out of thread or your machine will malfunction or you'll break a needle. There are two main parts to hems and finishes; the raw edge and the turned up portion. Most of the time, you'll finish the raw edge first to keep the fabric from unraveling or curling, and then you'll do the actual hemming, aka stitching that shit in place.

In a perfect world, hemlines are marked by a friend while you're wearing it. But ice cream has calories, so the world isn't perfect. How do you hem something all by your lonesome? Try the garment on while wearing whatever shoes or belt might go with it, and put a few guestimate pins in, turning the fabric underneath. After taking it off, finish pining all the way around the hem, and put it back on. This may take a couple rounds of try-on, pin, try-on, but cool your fucking jets - good things take time. When in doubt, take the safe route and hem it longer, as you can always shorten it. If you're still undecided or frustrated, the basting stitch from page 25 might come in handy.

Tips for getting your head around hemming:

- ✓ Match your thread color to the fabric as closely as possible

- ✓ The type of fabric determines the width of the hem - the lighter the fabric, the skinnier the hem width

- ✓ Save your own ass and practice your hem on a scrap of fabric first

- ✓ Iron that shit flat when you're finished

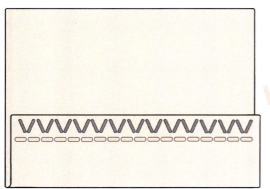

edge finish

hem turn-up

Just a Few Hem Options

Pinked-and-Stitched

If your fabric doesn't fray and isn't stretchy, the easiest hem is good ol' pinked-and-stitched; clean up the cut edge with either scissors or pinking shears, and then top-stitching the hem in place. If you hate the cut edge showing, you can also turn the edge under and stitch near the folded over edge.

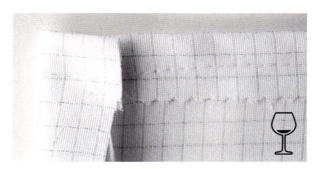

Finish and Top-Stitch

Finish the cut edge any way your heart desires - a simple zig-zag is the easiest and good for knits - and then top-stitch that shit down. If your fabric is stretchy, you'll need a double- or triple-straight stitch to preserve stretchiness.

Twin Needle

This is by far the best hem stitch for knits and other stretchy stuff. The twin needle makes two lines of stitching on the top, and then a zig-zag on the bottom to hold the hem and finish at the same time. You'll turn the hem up underneath and stitch from the right side of the fabric - enjoy feeling like a badass when this hem is done.

Narrow Hem

The narrow-hem foot can smell fear, but it is the best way to hem lightweight, dainty shit. Don't be scared of narrow hemming, but do practice before attacking your garment, and make sure your needle is sharp and ready for battle.

Blind Stitch

"Blind stitching is a bitch.", said every beginner seamstress, probably. This 'invisible' hem is useful on all sorts of garments and fabrics, and is explained more on the following page.

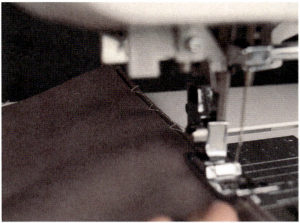

Blind Stitching

Your machine will have a dedicated 'blind stitch', and possibly a special blind stitch foot. Refer to your handy-dandy manual for the actual machine stitch, with these helpful-ass tips.

The two confusing parts of blind stitching are how the heck you're supposed to fold your fabric, and how to feed the fabric through the machine for the actual stitching.

Step 1
Finish the raw edge first - Team Lazy goes for the easy zig-zag stitch.

Step 2
Fold the hem under and, if you're really nervous, baste stitch it in place about an inch below the raw edge (page 25).

Step 3 (Headache #1)
Wrapping your mind around this fold - the hem will go under the main fabric, with the finished edge peeking out.

Step 4 (Headache #2)
The stitchline will be along the finished edge, with the zig-zag barely catching the main fabric.

From the right side of the fabric, you'll see spaced-out, single stitches keeping the hem in place. Practice the zig-zag catch several times before using it - the trick is actually getting the main fabric fold, but not so much that the fabric bunches or the stitch is long. In the image to the right, the first three stitches caught too far into the main fabric, and the last three stitches perfectly caught just the edge of the fold.

Curved Hems

Sewing a curved hem isn't hard but it's annoying as hell, because there's more fabric folded under than at the hemline. Baste stitching close to the hemline before actually hemming can make wrangling the excess-fabric easier.

Pin the underside fabric into small pleats, careful not to make the tucks so big that ironing the hem flat will make a visible corner in the fabric.

Here are two simple options to try:

Make a long, loose straight stitch close to the bottom, and then tug at every few stitches to lightly 'gather' the extra fabric into submission.

Option #1

Option #2

Making Bias Tape

Bias tape is most commonly used for finishing collars or sleeveless armholes - a strip of fabric encases the cut edge for a neat finish without having to 'turn under' the fabric. The lazy way to make bias tape is drive to the store and just friggin' buy some. This shows how to make bias tape when it's 2:00 am and you're out of gas and you have a god-like level of determination.

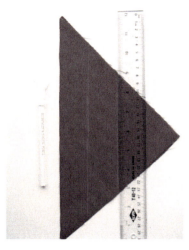

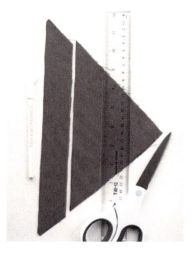

Make bias tape using the diagonal of your fabric. Why? I don't fucking know - something about the diagonal preserving stretch.

You'll want the flattened bias strip to be four times as wide as it will be when folded - take note that bias strips are a headache if made too skinny.

Chances are you won't have enough fabric along one diagonal to make the full bias strip, so you'll want to make a few to sew together.

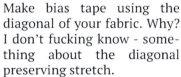

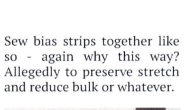

Bias strips are a helluva-lot easier to work with when ironed into shape. Fold the ends inward once and press, leaving a teeny tiny space in the middle.

Fold the bias tape in half and iron again - now this is the strip you'll use to 'encase' the cut edge like on page 20 or 65.

Sew bias strips together like so - again why this way? Allegedly to preserve stretch and reduce bulk or whatever.

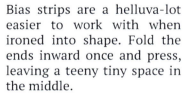

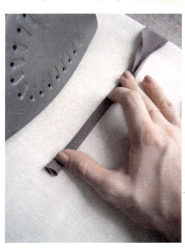

time to sew some shit

Making a Garment

Using a pattern is cool. Making it up as you go is cool, too. Whether you're a Pattern Princess or a a Do-It-Yourself Duchess, I've got your back. This section explains what the hell a pattern is, how to use one, and how to make one yourself using your own clothes as a guide.

What measurements are most important for buying or making a pattern? How to use as little fabric as posible? I'll show the basic patterns for most garments, and the order in which shit is usually put together. Are the patterns shown here the law of the land? Hell no - there are endless ways to alter, adjust, add-to, and arrange patterns to make them your own. The hope is that once you have the foundation, you can build your sewing empire from there. So gather all the king's horses and all the king's men, we're putting together garments!

Getting Your Motherfucking Measurements

You need to know your measurements when shopping for pre-made patterns, estimating fabric purchases, and especially when sewing more fitted clothing. One of the most important things I've learned while sewing is that size really is just a fucking number. Sizing differs between patterns, clothing companies, and the phases of the goddamn moon, so, while it's important to know your measurements, don't get wrapped up in them. You are a goddess made mortal and don't you ever forget it.

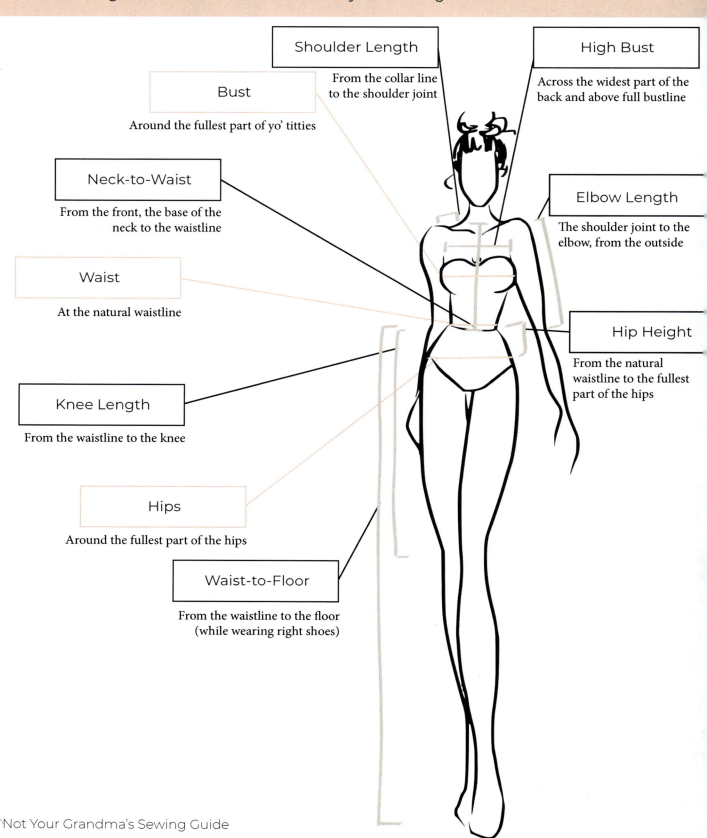

Shoulder Length
From the collar line to the shoulder joint

High Bust
Across the widest part of the back and above full bustline

Bust
Around the fullest part of yo' titties

Neck-to-Waist
From the front, the base of the neck to the waistline

Elbow Length
The shoulder joint to the elbow, from the outside

Waist
At the natural waistline

Hip Height
From the natural waistline to the fullest part of the hips

Knee Length
From the waistline to the knee

Hips
Around the fullest part of the hips

Waist-to-Floor
From the waistline to the floor (while wearing right shoes)

The main measurements you'll need to know are bust, waist, and hip,

as those are what patterns tend to list for sizing. Something to note; in sewing circles, the term 'Miss' or 'Misses' refers to regular, full-grown women, seemingly interchangeably with 'Woman'.

I promise you, trying to measure yourself is awkward and inaccurate, so have a friend measure you while you stand in a normal, relaxed posture.

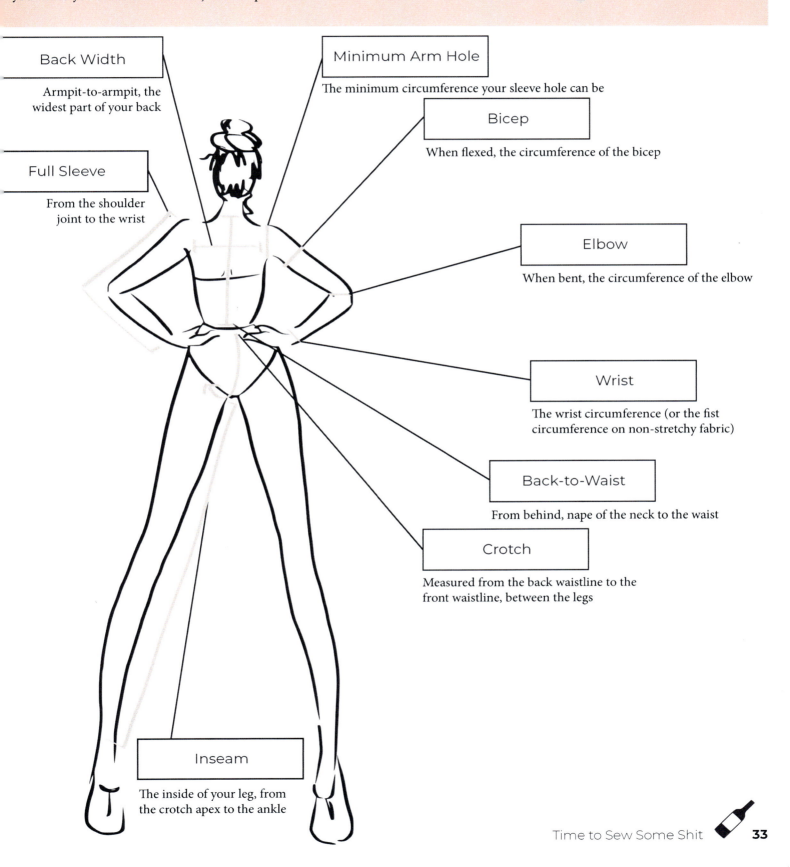

Back Width

Armpit-to-armpit, the widest part of your back

Full Sleeve

From the shoulder joint to the wrist

Minimum Arm Hole

The minimum circumference your sleeve hole can be

Bicep

When flexed, the circumference of the bicep

Elbow

When bent, the circumference of the elbow

Wrist

The wrist circumference (or the fist circumference on non-stretchy fabric)

Back-to-Waist

From behind, nape of the neck to the waist

Crotch

Measured from the back waistline to the front waistline, between the legs

Inseam

The inside of your leg, from the crotch apex to the ankle

Using a Pattern

The word 'pattern' can refer to two things; the actual pieces of fabric that make a garment, and all of the instructions that go into making that shit a reality. I will use the two randomly at my will and you will just have to keep the fuck up.

Pre-Made Motherfucking Patterns

Pre-made patterns are glorious gifts from the sewing gods, especially for beginners. There is virtually no guesswork involved from buying fabric all the way to finishing the hem. If you're all shiny and brand-new to sewing, starting off with a pre-made pattern would be an excellent use of that $8 left on your gift card.

Here are the most praiseworthy parts of a pre-made pattern to keep your eye out for:

Suggested Fabrics
While you don't have to strictly stick to the suggested fabrics, take note of how stretchy the pattern is expecting the fabric to be. Do they suggest a knit but you found a linen you love? Go up a size or two when cutting out the pattern to account for the lack of give.

Difficulty Levels
Patterns will give the down-low on what you're getting yourself into. Stay woke.

Symbol Guide
The specific symbols used in sewing differ slightly from company to company, but they will usually explain the relevant heiroglyphic-looking nonsense.

Pattern Pieces
It's helpful as fuck to know what the pattern pieces will look like before you start cutting/taping/crying. Keep in mind, some patterns have multiple variations of garments, and not all pieces will be needed for your specific project.

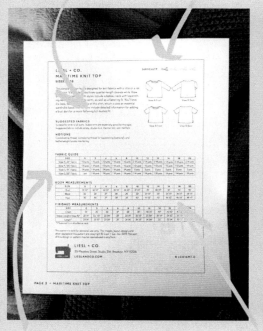

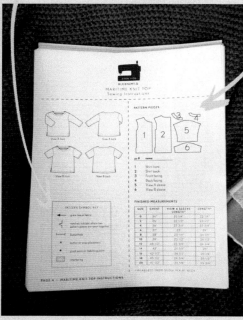

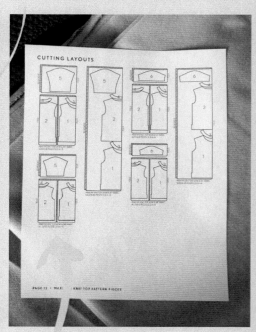

Yardage Purchasing Chart
While I provided a rough estimate of yardages on page 90, a pre-made pattern will tell you exactly what size fabric will fit their pieces. Add a little extra yardage if you pick a fabric with a 'right-way' pattern. Waste not, want not.

Suggested Size
Your measurements will let you know what size pattern to cut. Again, these differ wildly for God knows what reason, so always check.

Cutting Layouts
By far the most helpful part of a pre-sewing, be sure all of the pieces will fit on your fabric before you go snipping away.

Sewing Directions
If it's worth its salt (grandma expression), a pattern will include both written AND illustrated directions for putting together the garment. Take your time on each step; pick up your half-made garment and compare it with the pictures. Rip out shitty stitches. Look up words you don't know. You can do it as you, too, are worth your fucking salt!

Piecing Together a Pattern

Some patterns will come with nice, large pattern papers that you can cut-and-conquer, others you might have to print and/or piece together by your lonesome. While not difficult, it's not all-together intuitive sometimes.

Cut it.
Tape it.
Count it.

Step 1
Using the suggested size from the pattern instructions, cut out the pieces on their dotted lines.

Step 2
If the pattern must be pieced together, do your best to find the proper joining place. I fuck this up all the time and you will, too, so cheers to us.

Step 3
Make sure you have all pattern pieces cut out before tackling your fabric. Getting all of your pieces cut from the fabric just to realize you forgot the sleeves will drive you to drink.

Making A Pattern From Your Own Clothes

I'd love to tell you that there's a fool-proof way to make up a pattern using your own clothes; that there's a trick to getting the size right or how to visualize a pattern from a picture on Instagram. There's not. The truth is, I jumped in feet-first and figured it out as I went and, because of that, a lot of my early projects ended up in the giveaway pile or cut apart for later things. We're all just out here making up shit as we go along. For my kindred spirits who want to boldly take the hard road, here's a few tips for finagling your own patterns.

Start easy and loose (that's what she said).
Your first projects won't be perfectly fitted, so start with simple clothes that are loose or stretchy, like pajama pants or t-shirts.

Know the basic pattern pieces.
In this section, you can find the general shape of the pattern pieces for most garments. Having a general guide is helpful, because shit like sleeves and pant-crotch-areas are often not as they appear.

Fold in half wherever possible.
If you're going to fuck up the sleeve hole, it may as well be equally wrong on both sides. Folding a pattern in half when tracing and cutting at least guarantees your garment is symmetrically shitty.

Trace it out on paper.
This will help tremendously when getting a sense for the pattern shapes. Pin your folded garment right to the paper to keep it in place, especially when tracing curves.

Leave space for seam allowance and hems.
Don't trace right along a garment - leave space around the edge for where you'll actually sew the pieces together and hem - about ½" to 1". Always leave more space for hems than you think you'll want - many a project has gone the way of Goodwill because it ended up showing my cooch. Seam allowance size will change as you get used to sewing and find your preferences.

Account for darts (you advanced bitches).
As you get into more intricate, fitted clothing, you need to make note of any darts (page 82) and extra fabric you'll need when sewing.

fold in half

trace it out

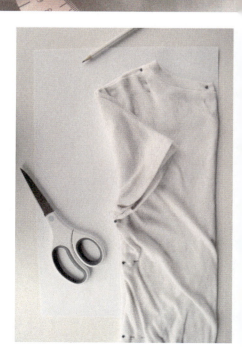

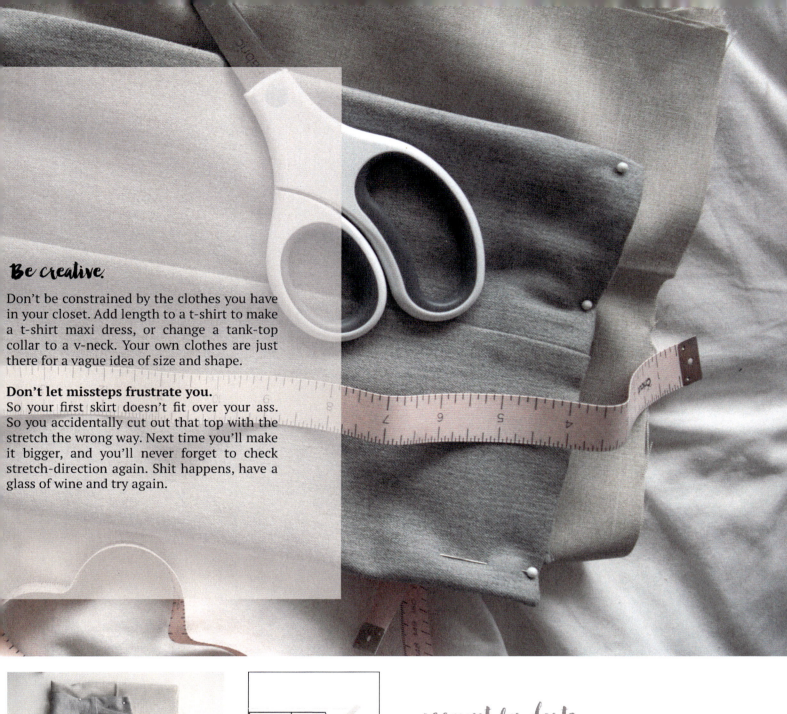

Be creative.

Don't be constrained by the clothes you have in your closet. Add length to a t-shirt to make a t-shirt maxi dress, or change a tank-top collar to a v-neck. Your own clothes are just there for a vague idea of size and shape.

Don't let missteps frustrate you.
So your first skirt doesn't fit over your ass. So you accidentally cut out that top with the stretch the wrong way. Next time you'll make it bigger, and you'll never forget to check stretch-direction again. Shit happens, have a glass of wine and try again.

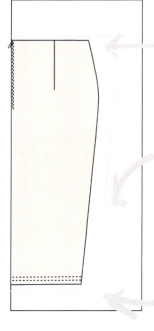

account for darts

leave space

Laying Out the Pattern on Fabric

Laying out a pattern on fabric is work of art in itself. You want to waste the least amount of fabric/money/fucks possible without having to run back to the store in shame to buy more. Take note of the following Q&A before you start slicing up fabric, even when using pre-made pattern layout suggestions.

Will your fabric shrink?
Wash and dry your fabric before doing any cutting.

Which way does the fabric stretch?
You want the most stretch to go horizontally across your chest and hips. You will forget to check this several times before making it a habit.

Is there a pattern or direction to the fabric?
Check the next page for help with napped, plaid, or other finicky fabrics.

Do you have a large work area?
A large, empty surface isn't necessary, but it sure fucking helps. Move your couch out of the way and work directly on the floor if you have to.

Is the pattern piece meant to be on the fold?
If you have half a pattern piece, it is meant to be placed right on the fold of a fabric so that, when it's cut out, you end up with one whole symmetrical piece.

Are you cutting from the wrong side of the fabric?
Pinning your pattern pieces to the wrong side of the fabric will allow you to put markings directly on the fabric. Can't tell which side is the 'right' side? Just pick one and stick to it.

Will all your pattern pieces fit?
Lay that shit out before you cut anything.

Is there another way to fit the pieces?
Welcome to adult-Tetris.

Will opposite pieces be...opposite?
At some point, you will cut out two left legs instead of a right and left leg. Ensure you're folding the fabric or pinning the pattern so that opposite pieces actually turn out facing opposite directions.

Is everything pinned down?
When it's all laid out, ensure your pieces are pinned directly to the fabric to keep them from sliding off.

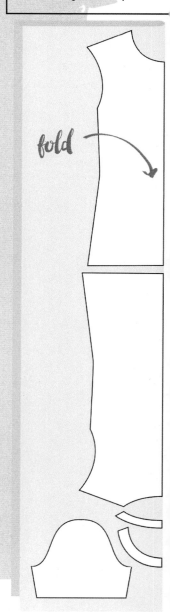

One Layout Option

fold

Tips for Directional Fabrics

Directional fabrics are any sort of fabric where the direction of the pattern piece actually matters. This includes striped and plaid fabrics, napped fabrics like velvet, shiny fabrics, fake fur, one-way print fabrics, and ribbed knits that have a definite grain.

Directional fabrics need to be cut out so that all of the pattern pieces' tops face the same direction. You may need to buy a little extra yardage of fabric to accommodate the layout. While extra care is needed in cutting out the pattern, prints do tend to hide stitching imperfections later on - silver lining.

On prints and patterns, pay attention to the 'centering' the front and back pattern pieces on the dominant vertical lines. Sleeves will lined up the same way, vertically. Go the extra mile to line up side seams, or pick an alternative direction for accents like pockets. It takes extra time but will give you a sick sense of satisfaction when you get it right.

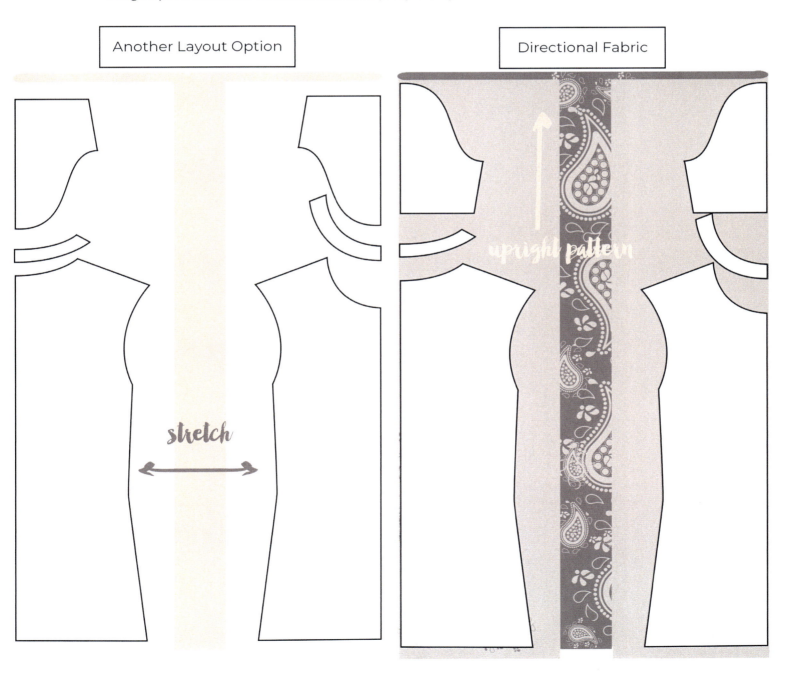

Cutting the Fabric Pieces

Cutting out pattern pieces is pretty straight-forward. FAPFSs have strict hand-to-Jesus techniques of 'only ever use the Pro-Cut Semi-Serrated Fabric 9000x', 'hold the fabric exactly like this', and 'make firm, 4.5" scissor strokes', but fuck that. Double- and triple-check that your pattern is pinned down securely and

just cut that shit.

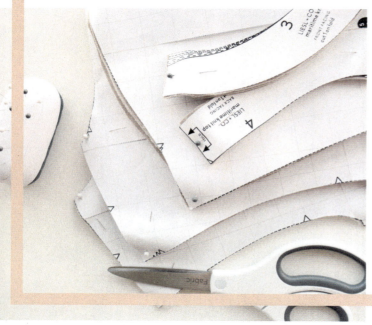

Save the excess fabric to test stitch tension and techniques on.

Keep your pattern pinned to your fabric until you need it, to make your life more zen and organized.

Transferring Pattern Markings

Pre-made patterns will come with a whole slew of markings to help you line up pieces properly, place buttons, and junk. There is an equally large number of ways to transfer those markings to the fabric after it's been cut out, but before you remove the pattern paper from the fabric. Always try to do marking on the wrong side of the fabric.

Snip   Cut small snips directly into the fabric, careful not to cut past the seam-line.

Chalk, pencil, or pen   Regular ol' pens and pencils work just fine for most fabrics, as long as none of your marks will show on the right side of the fabric. I will begrudgingly admit that special fabric chalks or pencils are useful for more sheer fabric or very dark fabrics.

Pins   Pins can be used as actual spot-holders or just as a way to lift up the pattern paper and mark underneath. Use pins sparingly when working with delicate shit.

Basting   **(Not shown, because it's so much extra work)** If you desperately need the markings on the right side of the garment, you can make a line of basting stitches through the pattern paper and the fabric. Gently tear and pull the pattern paper off once your precious overachieving is done.

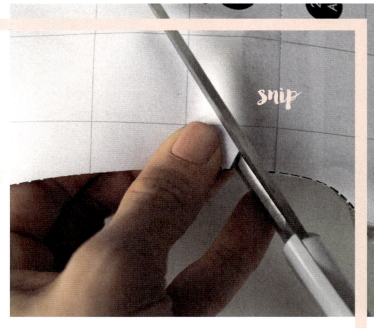

snip

pen

pins

However, don't let perfectionism become an excuse for never getting started.

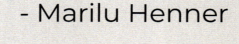

- Marilu Henner

Not Your Grandma's Sewing Guide

Putting Together a Goddamn Garment

This is what you came here for - making an original mother-fucking piece of clothing. The rest of this section will lay out garments' patterns, steps, tips and tricks. The basic diagrams will not include every possible garment variation - that would be berzerk. In-depth descriptions of fun additional things like elastic or t-shirt pockets can be found in the next section.

No matter what you're making, this is the general recipe:

1) Know all zippers, pockets, buttons, darts, and other shit you want to include beforehand

2) Cut out all of your pattern pieces

3) Stitch seams in the recommended order

4) Try on continuously as you sew to check the fit

5) Rip out shitty seams and redo when needed

6) Finish hems and edges at the end

Unsure how something will fit and don't want to waste expensive fabric? Buy a super-cheap fabric with similar stretch to test your pattern. Better to waste the extra time adjusting seams on muslin than to end up with a heap of ill-fitting, ruined silk.

If you know you want to lazy-finish all of your edges, do so before any other sewing is done. Pink or zig-zag stitch each pattern piece edge (page 17) before sewing it all together.

Understanding the Illustrations

No illustration, photograph, or video will be able to perfectly explain certain aspects of sewing something together. You've got to get your hands in there and try it out and swear and make mistakes. If a diagram is confusing the hell out of you, the internet is waiting with 1,000 different more-detailed tutorials.

Lighter shades will be the 'wrong' side of the fabric.

Darker shades will be the 'right' side of the fabric.

Seams (page 16) and seam finishes (page 19) are shown together as one step.

Hems and edge finishes shown with turned-up edges.

The Basic Top

A basic top - basically the most basic skill on which to build your base. No matter what shape, fabric, or sleeve-length you have in mind, making a top follows this same simple recipe. The sewing instructions are easy to follow and wrap your mind around, making it an excellent first project to dip into. So go ahead, be a basic bitch.

The Pattern

Front
- Usually a deeper neckline
- Often a little shorter than the back at the shoulder
- When cutting the pattern, account for any darts your boobs might need (page 82)

Back
- Higher neckline
- Sleeve hole may be deeper than the front

Two Sleeves
- Details about sleeve shapes found on next page
- Sleeve 'bell' length should equal sleeve hole

Front and Back Collar
- Collar options found on page 64
- Front and back shoulder widths must be equal
- Front and back side seams must be equal

Feeling lazy? Cut out two 'back' pattern pieces and then make the collar of one a bit deeper. Boom.

Alterations

The basic top pattern can be altered for any sleeve length, neckline, or hem length and still follow the same instructions. Shown are just a few ways the basic top pattern pieces can be altered - don't be afraid to get creative.

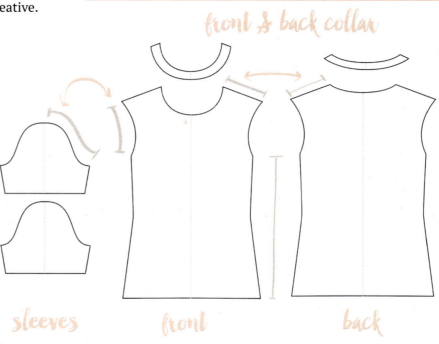

front & back collar

sleeves   front   back

Steps

Step 1
With the front and back pattern pieces separate, add any darts (page 82), reinforcement stitching (page 25), and T-shirt pockets (page 69) you plan to incorporate.

Step 2
Connect the front and back pieces at the shoulders, always sewing with the 'right sides' of the fabric together (aka your seams will be on the inside once that motherfucker is flipped right-side-out). Be sure to sew all the way to the cut edge on these seams or you'll end up with holes at your shoulder joint and collar.

Step 3
Finish the collar (page 64). This part is damn near impossible once the sides have been sewn together.

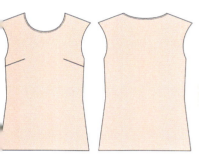

Sleeveless Top
Step 4 Sew that shit together at the sides.
Step 5 Finish the open edges (page 17).
Step 6 Hem (page 26) and call it a damn day.

Sleeve-d Top
Step 4 Find instructions for attaching sleeves on the next page, then attach some sleeves.
Step 5 Finish the sleeve edges.
Step 6 Hem it on up (page 26).

Accidentally make your first shirt too big? Just take it in at the side seams - quick and easy alteration spots are found on **page 88.** If your first try sucks, no one will say squat about your slightly crooked seams or imperfect hems, you wear that shitty shirt with pride.

Slay the Sleeve

Sleeves seem funky as hell at first, but you will pick them up quickly. Yes, you'll make sleeves that are too small. Yes, you'll pop a weak shoulder seam on a first date. But will you give up and live your life sleeveless? Hell no!

Sleeve Shape

Sleeves are actually cut in this weird fucking bell-shape. Don't think too hard about how it fits on the bodice, just go with it. I'm sure there's some exact way that FAPFSs make the bell curve, but toss that - fold it in half and make a nice sort-of 'S' shape.

Use your measurements from page 32 to decide how long to make the sleeve pieces, measured right down the center.

The top bell-curve of the sleeve should be the same length (or a teensy bit larger) as the sleeve-holes. To make sure your sleeve will fit comfortably, this length should a little bigger than the 'Minimum Arm Hole' from page 33. When in doubt, make it a little bigger than anticipated and take them in if you need to.

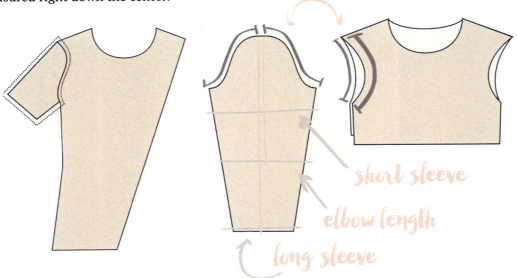

short sleeve

elbow length

long sleeve

Measuring the Armhole

Measuring around the curves is most easily done with flexible measuring tape before the shoulder seams are sewn. It doesn't have to be perfect, but you'd rather have the sleeve bell to be a little larger than the arm hole.

Did you fuck up and make your bell-curve-length too short? Cut into the curve dips ever-so-slightly to add to the perimeter. And you told yourself said you'd never use those high school geometry classes.

Steps

There are two equally-easy ways to attach sleeves to a bodice. When to finish the stupid cuff is entirely up to you - finishes are found on page 26. For fussy fabric or super small openings, finish the cuff *before* making the sleeve seam (as shown here). However, finishing the edge after the side seam is made will look cleaner. If you're unsure how long you want the sleeves, wait until both sleeves are fully attached to try on the top, pin, and finish.

Side Seam First

Step 1
Sew both side seams - make sure that stitch goes all way to the cut edge of the arm hole.

Step 2
Sew up the sleeve seam, double-checking that you're sewing the sleeve inside-out. Finish the cuff before or after making the sleeve seam.

Step 3
Flip the sleeve right-side-out, and insert it into the bodice as shown. Pin the sleeve opening to the bodice opening, and attach the sleeve in one circular stitch line.

Shoulder Seam First

Step 1
Pin the sleeve bell to the open bodice arc, making the right sides of the fabric kiss. This will look super weird and puckered when pinned, as the seam is on a curve.

Step 2
Sew the side seam and sleeve seam as one continuous line, pivoting at the armpit corner. Finish the cuff before or after making the long seam.

Sweatshirts

 All you fellow lazy-asses out there who live in sweatshirts and messy buns, this one's for you. A sweatshirt is the comfier cousin to the basic top - sweatshirt material is so fucking easy to work with, and the baggy fit makes sizing more of a vague guess than a precise idea. Take a crack at the crew-neck or up your game with a hoodie, then cozie up and keep it on for four days straight.

Base Pattern

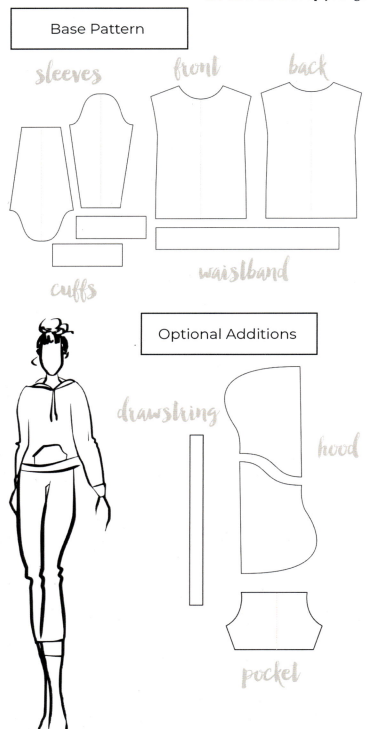

sleeves

front

back

cuffs

waistband

Optional Additions

drawstring

hood

pocket

The Pattern

Two Sleeves
- Details on sleeve shape found on previous page

Two cuffs (optional)
- If the material is stretchy, make the cuff small enough to comfortably slip your hand in and out
- Cuff length can be smaller than the sleeve wrist length

Front
- Usually a deeper neckline than the back
- Sleeve holes can be boxier than the basic top shape

Back
- Generally a higher neckline than the front
- More square shapes for sweatshirts are common

Waistband
- Waistband length can be smaller than the hemline, especially with a stretchier waistband fabric

Optional Crewneck Collar
- More details on crew neck collars found on page 64

Optional Hood Pieces
- There are umpteen hoodie variations out there, here's a very basic center-seam hood

Optional Front Pocket

Optional Drawstring for the Hood

Fabric

While there is actual sweatshirt material out there, any soft, knit fabric will suffice for the main sweatshirt pattern.

Looking for that stretchier, lined fabric you see on some sweatshirt cuffs, collars, and waists? It's called 'ribbed knit' and can usually be found in the same color as the main fabric. Any fabric (including the main fabric) can be used for cuffs and collars for different looks.

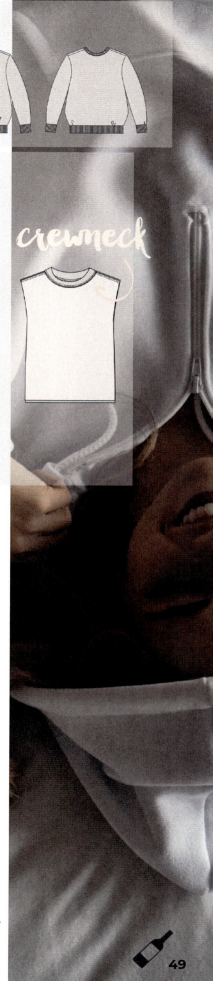

Steps

Step 1

Connect the front and back pieces at the shoulders, always sewing with the 'right sides' of the fabric together.

Step 3

Attach the sleeves using the directions on the previous page.

Step 4: Pocket

I like to wait until the sweatshirt is sewn together in case I've made it too long, but you can also attach the pocket earlier. **Turn** back the 'openings' of the pocket and **top-stitch** in place. **Pin** the pocket to the sweatshirt, lining up the bottom of the pocket with the hem. **Fold** the top and side edges under, and then **top-stitch** them to the front-piece fabric.

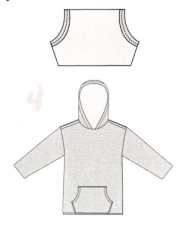

Step 2: Hood, Collar, Whatever

There are a hundred different patterns and ways to attach a damn hood - hop on the internet and find your favorite.

Connect the hood pieces down the 'back', taking care to sew all the way to the cut edge of the neckline.

Fold the front of the hood back, leaving room for a drawstring to be pulled through. Finish with a top-stitch or twin-needle stitch (page 25).

Pin the hood around the neckline and **attach**. If you're including a drawstring, you'll want to overlap the openings when pinning and only sew up to the open slots on each side.

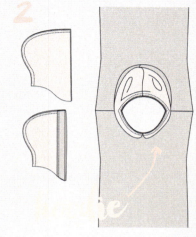

Find crew-neck and other collar instructions on page 64.

Step 5: Cuffs

Fold the cuff piece in half (hamburger-style?) and make a seam at the edge, creating a circular band. **Fold** the cuff band over, *right-side out*, and slip over the sleeve. **Pin** the cuff evenly to the sleeve - an easy trick is to pin four 'corners' of the cuff to the sleeve, and stretch between to evenly add pins around sleeve. **Attach** the cuff to the sleeve with one continuous seam. For stretchy cuffs, gently stretch the fabrics flat while you sew, and use a stitch for stretchy shit (page 12). Optionally, the sleeve edge can be finished like a normal shirt (page 17) or with elastic at the wrists (page 78).

Step 6: Waistband

The waistband will be attached exactly like a cuff. The bottom edge of the pocket will be sandwiched between the front fabric and the waistband, closing the bottom of the pocket. Make a seam along the edge, sewing through both layers of waistband, main fabric, and (at one point) pocket fabric. Boom. Yesterday you wanted a plain sweatshirt, and today you have a plain sweatshirt. Follow your dreams,.

Drawstring can be bought at a fabric store by the yard, or you can make your own fabric drawstrings on page 66.

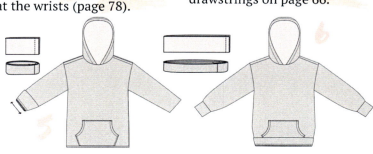

Pants and Shorts

Pants are a slight level-up from tops because of the stupid confusing crotch. As a beginner, Obstacle #1 is making a pant pattern that fits nicely. Your first pair will likely give you camel-toe, hug your upper thigh too tight, and bell-bottom at the ankle. It's an uphill battle to learn what measurements go where. Obstacle #2 is keeping your wits about you while navigating the actual sewing of the stupid crotch. Worry not, though, that's only two challenges - this is a mountain you can climb!

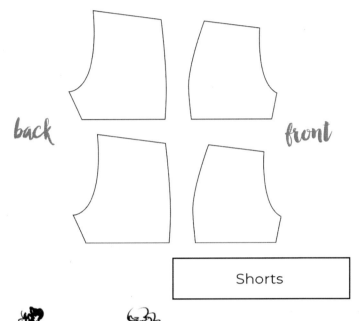

back · front

Shorts

The Pattern

The pattern for shorts and pants are the same - differing only at the hem length. If you're making your own pants pattern, a good pair of skinny jeans is an excellent template. Feeling extra ballsy and want to go by measurements? All leg, crotch, and waist measurements from page 32 will be needed to ensure a good fit.

For tight-fitting pants, like leggings, or men's pants, you might notice a small diamond of fabric right at the crotch apex. Google 'pants pattern with gusset' (which is a very funny word) for tutorials on incorporating it.

Left and Right Back
- The crotch 'J' is deeper than the front, to accommodate your amazing ass
- The waist slants upward slightly, warding off whale-tale
- Upper thigh is usually thicker than the front as well

Left and Right Front
- The front inseam and back inseam lengths must match
- The front and back side seam lengths must match

Pants

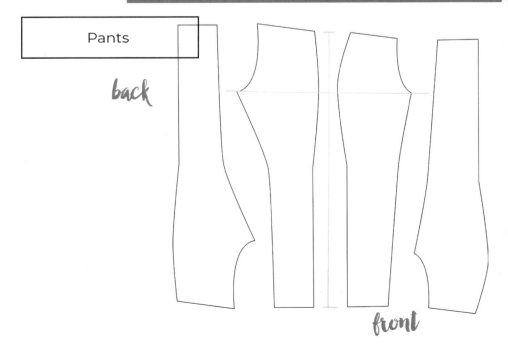

back · front

Steps

Step 1
Add whatever pockets you're planning to the front and back pieces. Quadruple-check which side of the fabric is the right side, which pieces are front and back, and which sides are right and left. Mark that shit on the wrong side with a pen if you need to.

Step 2
With right sides together, make a seam along the 'J's' of the front and back. Sew all the way to the inseam edge if you don't want a super-cute hole in the crotch.

Step 3
Pin the front half to the back half at the inseam, and sew one continuous seam from one ankle to the other. Add reinforcement stitching at the inseam V on top of the stitch line for extra security.

Step 4
Make side seams along both outer edges. Try on the pants at this point to see if they fit, and take it in where you need to. Pay attention to how the waist fits - taking pants in once the waistband is added is a real pain.

Step 5
Handle the waistband (page 66). If you forgot to account for the waistband you had your heart set on, that's A-okay. Roll with the punches and pick a new waistband.

Step 6
Try on and hem (page 26), and then take that sexy bum outside to show them off.

51

Skirts

If you look up the history of the skirt, you'll find that a skirt is the oldest form of clothing known to mankind. That old, and people still make skirts without pockets. There are a ton of ways to put together a skirt, none of which are too intimidating, but the dizzying amount of variations make it the most difficult sewing project to succinctly tutorialize. Nonetheless, we'll invent that wheel, discover fire, and, unlike primitive men, put pockets in our goddamn skirts.

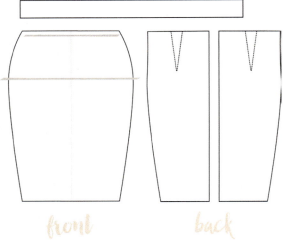

waistband

front   back

Pencil Skirt

The Pattern

This section will show the patterns and steps for sewing straight, pencil, and circle skirts. Make your projects easier by opting for one- or two-piece patterns with simple waistbands, or up your game with zippers, linings, and (hooray!) pockets.

Straight/Maxi Skirt
Matching Front and Back Piece
- Straight waistline cut
- Gently taper at bottom for room to walk
- Bottom hem could be cut straight or with a slight curve

Waistband Page 66

Pencil Skirt
Front
- Waistline is usually fitted
- Hip curve depends on hip measurement

Back (One Piece or Seperated)
- One piece, if the zipper will be added to the side seam
- Split into two pieces for back-centered zippers
- Must add length to the top to account for darts. I don't care how flat your ass is, you'll want darts in a pencil skirt. Measuring for dart size is on page 82.

Waistband or Waistband Lining Page 66

Circle Skirt
- Literally, just a circle of fabric with a waistband. Details for circle skirt pattern-making on the next page.

Straight/Maxi Skirt

waistband

front & back

Circle Skirt

Circle skirts usually come in three variations of fullness - full, three-quarters, and half. How much fabric you use dictates how voluptuous and twirl-worthy your skirt will be, and how you go about cutting the pattern.

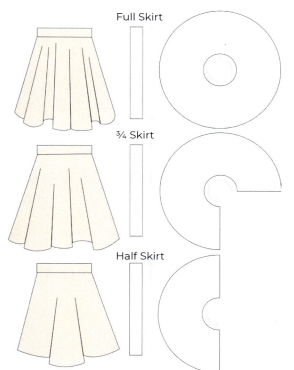

Full Skirt

¾ Skirt

Half Skirt

Motherfucking Circle Math

Disclaimer: for virtually any other type of clothing, you can draft your own patterns by laying your own clothes down and tracing them. Circle skirts, however, come from their own special circle of hell. Truly (irritatingly), the easier way to make a pattern is with math.

For any skirt size, you will have a waistband piece that fits your waist measurement. The inner arc of the circle fabric will need to be at least as long as your waist measurements to ensure it wraps all the way around. The outer arc of the circle fabric will be determined by how long you want the skirt.

So how the frack do you figure out the actual measurements? Here's that high school geometry again. You'll use your waist measurement (circle circumference) to calculate the radius of the inner arc using the below calculations (If you want your skirt to include gathers or pleats, page 80, add a few inches):

Full Skirt	Waist / 2π
¾ Skirt	Waist * $\frac{2}{3}$ / π
Half Skirt	Waist / π

The outer arc of the skirt will be the radius plus the skirt length you have in mind. Measure from the fold corner and mark out an arc along the fabric. Whew. Deep breath. You can do this.

Cutting the Stupid Circle

There's a handy trick to cutting out half and full circle skirts as one piece. For the half skirt, fold your fabric in half and make your measurements along the fold.

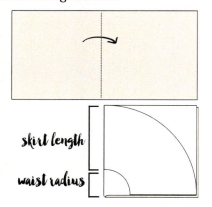

skirt length

waist radius

With a full circle skirt, you'll fold the fabric twice (as shown), and make your measurements along the double-fold. When cut out, the fabric will be one continuous piece with no side seam. If you plan to add a zipper or pockets, you'll have to cut one or both side seams - but this way of drafting ensures the skirt is even all the way around.

General-ish Skirt Steps

No matter what your skirt will look like, this is the basic order-of-operations to follow. Skip the shit you're not incorporating, and take your time to look at each step.

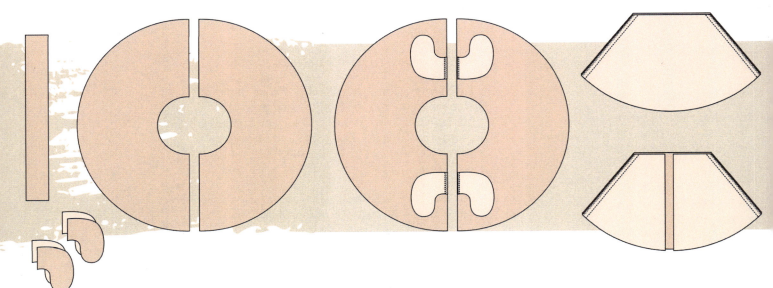

Step 1
Cut out all pattern pieces beforehand, including pockets and waistbands. A prepared bitch is a stress-free bitch.

Step 2
Attach your pocket pieces to the main fabric, whichever style you opt for (page 68).

Step 3
If you're not using a zipper, sew up all open side seams.
If you are including a zipper, keep one seam un-sewn. Did you cut one continuous full skirt piece but plan on including a zipper? You'll need to cut an opening all the way up one spot of the skirt fabric.

God bless pockets.

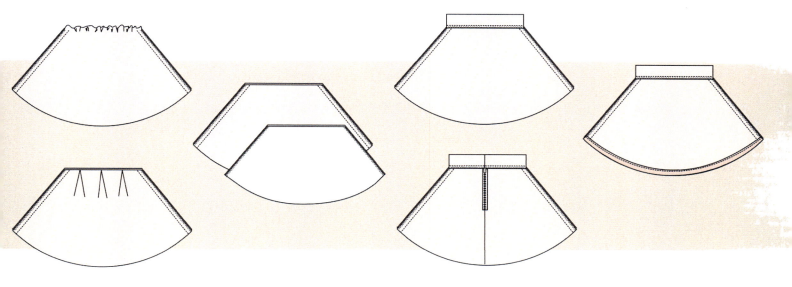

Step 4
Create any pleats or gathers (page 80).

Step 5
Add lining (page 55).

Step 6
Finish the waistband (page 66) and zipper (page 70). Pay attention to what you want for the final waistband/zipper situation as that determines which comes first.

Step 7
Try on and hem (page 26).

Pencil Skirt Steps

While the steps for creating a pencil skirt aren't terribly different from any other skirt, sometimes it's helpful to see a variation. This variation shows a waistband lining; it's not a full lining, but the waist edge will be finished nicely with no visible topstitching.

Step 1
Create darts on the back piece or back panels (page 82).

Step 2
Sew all side seams except the seam for the zipper.

Step 3
Flip the skirt right-side out, and pin the waistband lining (wrong-side out) to the top. Sew the lining to the skirt at the top edge.

Step 4
Insert the zipper per the zipper-with-lining steps on page 70.

Step 5
For added flair (and room for your knees to waddle), leave a couple inches at the bottom of the zipper seam open. Top-stitch the seam down around the opening.

Step 6
Try it on and decide if you want to take it in around the knees. With a close-fitting skirt, it's tough to judge the fit until the zipper is installed. The side seams can be gently tapered at the bottom without fucking up the top, and go ahead with the hem when it fits nicely.

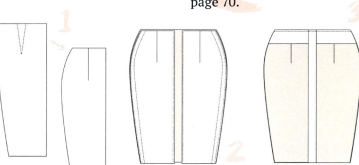
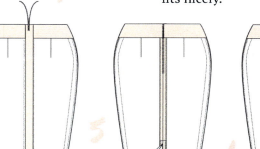

One-Piece Dresses

 The person who decided a long t-shirt was an okay excuse to not wear pants deserves to have a statue erected. Here, when I say a 'one-piece dress', I mean that the bodice and skirt are cut as one continuous piece - there's no seam at the waist connecting a 'top half' and a 'bottom half'. Shift dresses, sheath dresses, and some maxi dresses are cut out this way; they're easy, dressed-up or down, and, hey, no pants necessary.

sleeves

front & back collar

front   back

The Pattern

The pattern for a one-piece dress is just the pattern for a top with a longer hem (page 44). Not fucking kidding. For more fitted one-piece dresses, like a sheath dress, the pattern might be cut with some curves on the side, à la the pencil skirt pattern shape (page 52).

The pattern may widen slightly at the bottom, depending on fabric and the shape you're going for. 'Just how wide?' is something you'll learn to gauge the more you sew.

Front
- Usually a deeper neckline
- Account for any darts your tatas might need (page 82)
- If you're including lining, you'll have a second front piece cut from your lining fabric (page 84)
- Shoulders and side seams measurements should line up between the front and back piece just like the basic top

Back
- Usually a higher neckline
- Possibly deeper arm holes
- If you're including lining, you'll have a second back piece cut from your lining fabric
- If you're adding a zipper, your back piece will be cut in half (add an extra ½" to each side to account for the zipper seam)

Two Sleeves
- Sleeve shape and measuring found on page 46

Collar Finishes
- If you're not including lining, you'll need the pieces for your collar of choice (page 64)

For one-piece dresses with lining, check out page 84.

Steps

If your dress won't have any fancy additions, like lining or a zipper, follow the steps for making a basic top (page 44). The instructions here will help you navigate the more ballsy designs.

Step 1
Make any darts on the front piece (page 82), and add pockets to the front and back (page 68).

Step 2
Sewing with right sides to-gether, connect the front to the back at the shoulders.

Step 3
Either finish the collar (page 64) or add lining (page 84). This is a good time to try on and fix anything hat you don't love. If you can't get your head through the stupid neckhole, for example, all is not lost - just add a zipper in.

Step 4
Attach the sleeves or finish the raw edge (page 46)

Step 5
Optionally install the zipper (page 70). If your back piece was whole, cut a line straight up the center. Don't try to cut 'just where the zipper will go' - it looks wonky as hell.

Step 6
Try on and hem (page 26).

Two-Piece Dresses

Two-piece dresses take time, patience, a plan, and roughly four bottles of wine to get through, but make you feel like a badass to finish. A two-piece dress is any sort of dress with a distinct top half and bottom half, that are connected at the waist with a seam. Don't shy away from the extra steps - embrace your inner overachiever and get to work.

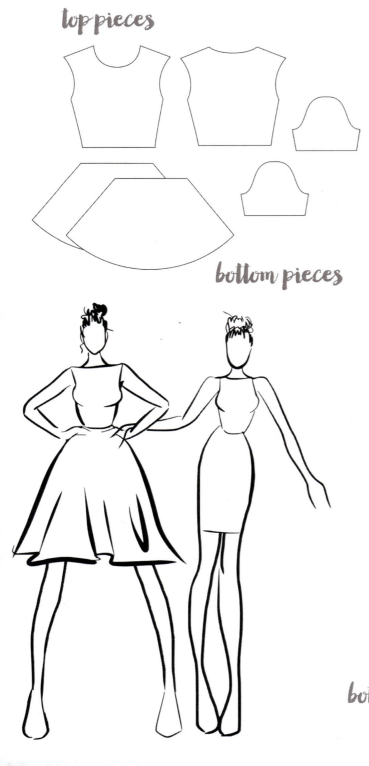

top pieces

bottom pieces

The Pattern

A two-piece dress pattern is just any sort of top pattern (page 44) combined with any sort of bottom pattern. I swear to God, that's it. No special techniques or pattern pieces, just a top and a bottom.

Top Pattern
- The only difference to make note of for a two-piece dress top is that the hem usually stops at the waist, and is more fitted around the waist.
- If you're using your own clothes to make up a pattern, a fitted t-shirt pinned up at your natural waist will give a good idea of the bodice shape.

Bottom Pattern
For some reason, my first few two-piece dresses came out too short. Add a couple extra inches of hem when making your pattern to keep your cooch covered.

Lining Pattern
If you're adding lining, you'll need top and bottom pieces cut from your lining fabric. More info on linings at page 84.

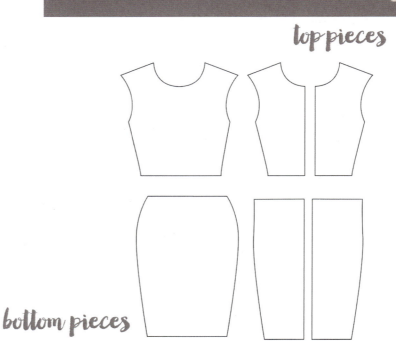

top pieces

bottom pieces

Because of the extra pattern pieces, making a two-piece dress will seem hella daunting. Adding in more moving parts, like lining and zippers, might just push you over the fucking edge. To help ease that anxiety, you'll find steps for different dress variations - take each step slowly and with a Xanax and you'll get through it just fine.

No Zipper, No Lining

 The most basic two-piece dress, without lining or a zipper, should be made from stretchy material or with a pattern wide enough at the waist to slip on and cinched with elastic or a tie.

Step 1
Fully construct a top without hemming the bottom (page 44). Likewise, sew your skirt without finishing the waistband or hemming (page 52). Try both halves on individually to make sure they fit how you'd like them to.

Step 2
Flip your skirt inside out and pin to the top's hem. Make one continuous seam along the waistline using a good stitch for stretchy stuff, or you'll end up with a super cute garment that you can't get on past your shoulders.

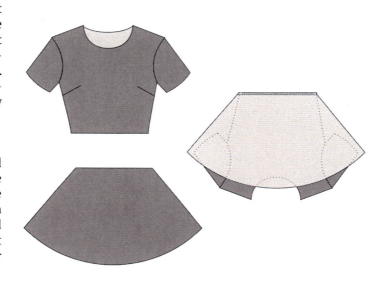

Step 3
If you're adding elastic, you'll attach it to the inside of the dress once the top and bottom are attached, either directly to the fabric or with the sheath method (page 78). There are sneakier ways to attach elastic, but this is a goddamn beginner's guide.

Step 4
Try on and hem. If you get this far and hate it, or it doesn't fit right, or it's too short, don't swear off two-piece dresses for good. Learn from your mistakes and tackle it again another time.

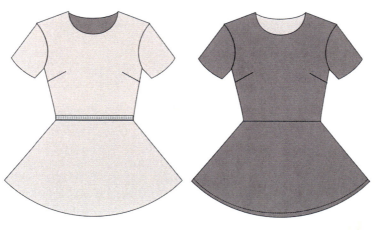

Adding Lining

Find more details about lining on page 84 - why you'd use it, what type of fabric to buy for it, and other helpful shit.

Not all two-piece dresses you make will need full lining.

Are you using lining just on top? Attach the lining to the top per usual (page 84), and then treat the top and lining as one piece when connecting the skirt.

Just using lining on the bottom? You'll connect your skirt and skirt lining to the top at once. If your fabric is slippery, baste stitch your lining to your skirt at the waist beforehand.

Adding A Zipper

If you're adding a zipper to the back of the dress, the back of both the top and bottom should be cut in half, adding ½" to 1" on both sides for the zipper seam. Don't try to cut the fabric 'just as far down as the zipper will go', installing the zipper is a thousand times harder and the end result looks wonky as hell.

Measure your needed zipper length before you buy that sucker, or you'll end up driving to the fabric store twice in one day. For fitted dresses, the zipper should extend far enough below the waistline to shimmy it over your hips or your shoulders. Pin the skirt hem together and test getting in and out of the dress.

No Zipper, With Lining

 When buying lining fabric for a two-piece dress with no zipper, check that the lining material is just as stretchy as the main fabric, lest it end up too stiff to slip on.

Step 1
Fully construct the top and top lining, and then attach the top lining - do not hem either (page 44). Sew the skirt and skirt lining, keeping them separate, and don't mess with the waist or hem of either bottom piece (page 52).

Step 2
Flip the main skirt inside-out and pin to the main top at the waist. Connect the main skirt to the top with one continuous seam around the waist, using stitches suitable for stretchy fabric. Be careful not to catch the top lining fabric.

Step 3
Flip the main fabric inside out so you're working with the 'right side' of the lining. Attach the lining skirt the same way you attached the main skirt, using stretchy seams when appropriate.

Step 4
If you're adding elastic, pull the lining out of the way and attach elastic to the inside of the main fabric (page 78). Since the lining will be 'hiding' the elastic, sewing directly to the main fabric is the laziest way to get the job done.

Lining usually serves two purposes: as a barrier for see-through main fabric, and to hide seams from view. Could you care less if the seams are visible inside? Skip Steps 2 and 3 and connect all four pieces at the waist seam.

Step 5
Try the dress on and hem both the lining and main fabric separately. Your lining will probably be hemmed a little shorter than your main fabric, but picking a pretty lining fabric and hemming it longer for a 'peek-a-boo' look is also cute as hell.

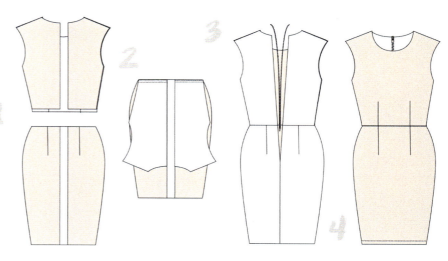

Step 1

Fully construct the top without installing the zipper or hemming the waist (page 44). Likewise, sew the skirt without installing the zipper, finishing the waist, or hemming the bottom (page 52).

Step 2

Pin the top and bottom at the waist and connect with a seam, making sure to sew with the 'right sides' of the pieces together.

Step 3

Install the zipper (page 70) like normal, treating the whole garment as one piece. Don't underestimate how far below the waistline your zipper should go - try the dress on after attaching the zipper, but before closing the back seam, as you might have to take it out and reinstall.

Step 4

Hem it all up and admire your handiwork. If you get this far and forgot to try on as you go, it's stupid simple to just flip the dress inside-out and take it in from the sides (instead of messing around more with the zipper).

With Zipper and Lining

This is the Holy Grail of beginner sewing projects. Every hefty sewing obstacle you could face, rolled into one adventure. If you've made it this far, you're up for a motherfucking challenge.

Step 1

Complete the top and top lining, connecting the two, but not hemming either one or installing a zipper (page 44). Sew the skirt and skirt lining, leaving the waists, hems, and zippers unfinished as well (page 52).

Step 2

Pin the main skirt and main top together at the waist and make a seam, sewing with the 'right sides' of the top and bottom pieces together.

Step 3

Pull the main fabric out of the way, and sew the lining skirt to the lining top at the waist.

For non-zippered two-piece dresses, you can cut corners by treating the linings and main fabrics as one. I don't suggest going that route for zippered dresses, as you'll end up with a wonky, super thick bulge where the zipper meets the waist.

Step 4

Install the zipper like normal (page 70), making sure the zipper extends far enough below the waistline to comfortably pull on. Try the dress on before finishing the lining or the back seam in case you need to redo anything.

Step 5

Try on, hem, and glory in the accomplishment of making the hardest garment a beginner sewer could tackle - you deserve a goddamn medal.

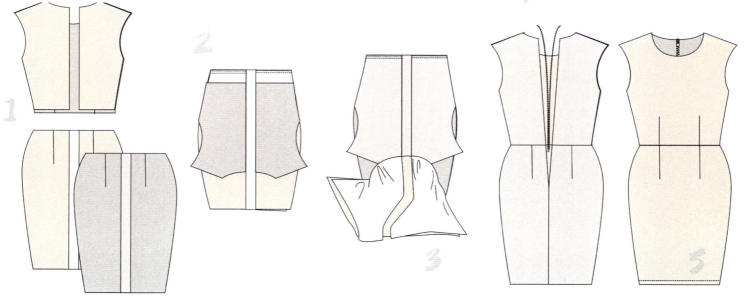

extra stuff

Odds and Ends and Add-Ons

If a basic pattern is the vanilla ice cream of a sewing sundae, then this section explains all of the delicious mix-ins at your fingertips. Buttons are your sprinkles, elastic is the hot fudge, and pockets are the motherfucking delicious cookie-dough pieces. Your project can be as simple or as elaborate as you want, depending on how many extra elements you're throwing in. My advice is to start with plainer projects and work your way to pineapple-upside-down-with-caramel-and-gummy-bears.

None of the extra elements are crazy complex, but they do require planning and a practice attempt or two. Know what shit you're adding in before you start sewing and put your damned pride aside to test on a scrap of fabric. There are different techniques for some elements and I encourage you to give each a taste. While your plain t-shirt or pajama shorts might be well-made, throwing in a little something extra could be the cherry on top.

Collar Finishes

Which collar finish to choose depends on collar shape, material, and whether or not you want visible stitches. Check out the pros and cons of each collar finish to decide which is right for your project.

Crewneck

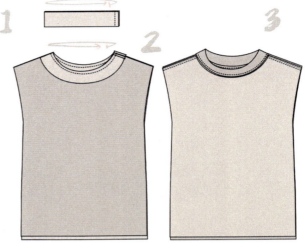

Pros
- Almost as easy as the fold-over method

Cons
- Can look fucked-up if done with the wrong material. Stick to using this on sweatshirts or other generously-soft fabric.

Step1
Measure the collar line and cut an equal length of fabric. Fold in half and make the collar seam on the 'wrong side' of the fabric.

Step 2
Pin your collar to the main fabric, right sides together. Make a line of stitches close to the collar line - this will become the 'collar seam' and the stitches will be hidden from the front.

Step 3
Fold your collar inward, pin, and topstitch below the collar seam, on the main fabric. Optionally, add a second line of decorative stitches above the collar seam for kicks.

Foldover and Topstitch

Pros
- Easy as fuck
- Great for athletic gear and stretchy material

Cons
- Cannot be used for stiffer fabrics
- Because the fabric is being pulled in a weird way, it puckers on rounded necklines

Step 1
Finish the edge with a zig-zag stitch (page 12) if you think the fabric might fray. You can't use a turned-and-stitched finish for these edges because the fabric just won't pull that way. You might also add reinforcement stitching (page 25) if you're worried about stretch over time.

For a v-neck, make a small snip into the 'v' corner before turning over the edge. Otherwise, the 'v' will have a dumb pucker.

Step 2
Fold the edge under and pin in place - use a bunch of pins if the fabric is being difficult.

Step 3
Top-stitch the foldover in place. For stretchy fabric, like on t-shirts, use a triple-stitch or twin-needle stitch.

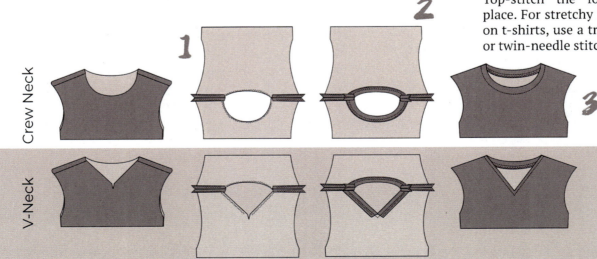

Bias Tape

Pros
- Good for fabric that won't fold over nicely

Cons
- Must buy or make bias tape that nicely compliments your main fabric

Step 1
Make or buy bias tape (page 29).

Step 2
The 'non-lazy approach' is to measure the collar and make a bias tape loop that perfectly fits. The lazy way is to just pin it around and not give a heck about where the exposed edges meet.

Step 3
Top-stitch in place. For v-necks, pull the 'V' into a straight line and add bias tape directly across - snipping into the 'V' corner of the main fabric will help.

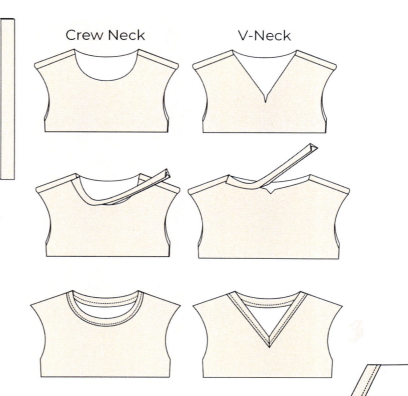

Crew Neck   V-Neck

V-Neck Finish
To finish a v-neck, fold the 'V' in half from the inside and make one short seam where the 'V' meets.

Facing

Facings are my favorite way to finish a collar. They look the best and honestly maybe take five extra minutes to whip together. The collar of garments with full-lining (page 84) would be look the same when complete.

Pros
- The only finish that doesn't show stitches at the neckline
- No awkward puckering of the fabric
- Works well with any type of material

Cons
- The pattern takes maybe two minutes longers to cut out. That's it - there's no other reason to shy away from it.

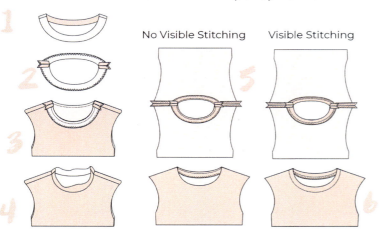

No Visible Stitching   Visible Stitching

Step 1
Cut out pattern pieces that match the shape of the bodice neckline - this is honestly the most annoying step. Can be as thin as 1" wide for knit fabrics, but should be thicker with bulkier materials. Connect the two pieces at the 'shoulder'.

Step 2
If your fabric might fray or stretch, finish the outer edge with a zig-zag stitch. Not needed for knits, but it looks nice as fuck.

Step 3
Pin the facing onto the bodice so the 'right sides' are together. Make a continuous stitch line close to the edge.

Step 4
Flip the facing inward.

Step 5
If you don't want any stitches to show on the outside, you'll make straight-stitch on the facing, 'catching' the two seam allowances underneath (the main fabric seam allowance and the facing seam allowance), but **don't** stitch through the main fabric. Doing this keeps the facing from flopping up and over.

If you like seeing the stitches from the outside for detail, just topstitch the facing right to the main fabric.

Step 6
I know it's annoying, but take 43 seconds to iron the collar flat at the end. It looks much better and keeps the facing in place.

Waistbands

If you forget to account for a waistband when making your pattern, it's insanelyl easy to throw it in on the fly. These waistband techniques work for skirts, pants, and shorts, so don't discriminate. When cutting out the waistband piece, take note of the stretch direction and pattern of the fabric.

Foldover and Topstitch

The easiest waistband to sew - make just a teeny foldover, or a little thicker to look more like an honest-to-god waistband.

Step 1
Finish the cut edge of the waistband with something suited to stretchy fabrics, like a zig-zag (page 12).

Step 2
Fold the waistband over. If you want to add elastic into the sleeve, different elastic styles are found on page 78.

Step 3
Topstitch the waistband down with a stretchy stitch.

Foldover with Drawstring

Adding drawstrings in that sucker, like for pajama pants?

Step 1
Finish the raw edge of the skirt and cut a slit in the waistband where the drawstrings will be pulled through. Put a teeny tiny stopper-stitch under the slit to keep it from stretching.

Step 2
Fold the waistband over - don't try to sew the waistband down with the drawstring inside the sleeve; sage-as-fuck advice.

Step 3
Topstitch the fold down. Find instructions for making your own drawstrings below.

Making Straps

Spaghetti straps, drawstrings, other decorative shit - you can buy all of these in the fabric store, or go the extra mile to make them yourself from scraps of fabric. How thin you can make a strap depends entirely on how thick the fabric is, so test out some mini straps before going all-in on your last shreds of material.

Fold-Over
This strap is so easy for pajama bottom drawstrings and other casual fabrics that won't fray at the edge.

Fold the fabric in half and make one seam down the edge. Pinning the fold in place really helps keep the strap from flattening out in the machine.

Stitched-and-Turned
Don't want a visible stitch line? Pick this strap. Exactly how skinny you can make a stitched-and-turned strap depends on fabric and will take practice.

Pin in half, 'wrong side' out. Make a stitch along the edge, leaving enough space to flip the strap, and turn.

 Amateur-tip, use a safety pin to pull the strap inside-out.

Bias-Tape
If you are worried about the cut edge of the fabric fraying, you'll make a strap the same way you would make bias tape (page 29).

Fold of edges inward, and then fold the piece in half again. You'll end up with the cut edges tucked inside - but be careful not to make it too bulky. Stitch the fold closed.

Fold-Over

Stitched-and-Turned

Bias-Tape

Circular Waistband

This waistband is useful for stretchy shit, or if made big enough to fit elastic. How the hell else are you going to get it on?

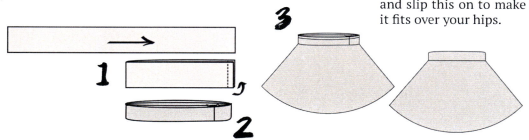

Step 1
Fold the fabric piece *wrong-side* out, to make a seam.

Step 2
Fold the waistband over, *right-side out* this time, and slip this on to make sure it fits over your hips.

Step 3
Pin the waistband to the skirt, upside down, lining up the cut edges. Use a stretchy stitch to sew through the main fabric and both waistband ends.

Use page 78 to add elastic into your super cute new waistband. Throw a drawstring in there by cutting a slit in the waistband, or not fully connecting the fabric loop in the first step.

Waistband with Zipper

You don't need a waistband to install a zipper into bottoms - any damn zipper technique from page 70 will do just fine without one. This technique is just the prettier way to hide the ugly zipper edges inside the waistband.

Step 1
Your skirt or pants should have one seam left open for the zipper, and the waistband piece should be thick enough to fold in half.

Step 2
Pin the waistband to the main fabric, 'right sides' together, and connect with a seam.

Step 3
Install the zipper using any technique from page 70 - the zipper should stop halfway up the waistband, so that it can be folded over.

Step 4
(This part will seem confusing but roll with it.) Fold the waistband so that it's inside out. Optionally fold up the bottom to hide the raw edge.

Step 5
Make a line of stitches inside the zipper line. Your brain will say, 'But then the zipper will be stuck on the outside!', but you tell your brain to shut up and give it a go.

Step 6
Flip the waistband right-side out. The zipper will be in the right place, all cozy and secure inside the waistband. goddamn magic.

Step 7
Optionally stitch the bottom edge of the waistband in place - most of the time this is done just below the seam, or right on top of the seam. (FAPFSs would say 'in the ditch').

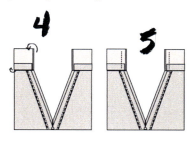
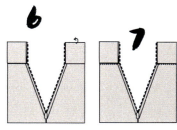

Waistband with Zipper and Hooks

This waistband can be added after the zipper is fully installed, which is good in case you straight up forgot about it.

Step 1
The waistband piece should be slightly longer than your waist, as the hook or button will need an overlapping flap.

Step 2
Pin the waistband to the main fabric, 'right sides' together, with one edge over-shooting the main fabric. Attach the waistband with a seam near the cut edge.

Step 3
Flip the garment around and fold the waistband inside-out.

Step 4
Sew a short stitch at the ends of both sides of the waistband.

Step 5
Cutting off the corner edge makes for a sharper point once the waistband is flipped. Get that bulk out of the heckin' way.

Step 6
Turn the waistband right-side-out. Fuckin' beautiful.

Step 7
Optionally stitch the bottom edge of the waistband in place - most of the time this is done just below the seam, or right on top of the seam.

Step 8
Attach hooks (page 77) or a button (page 76).

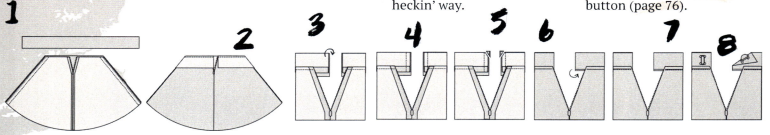

Pockets Pockets Pockets Pockets Pockets

Pockets - the single greatest goddamn thing to ever happen to clothing. The Statue of Liberty needs pockets, pockets must be a constitutional right, and we should add a pocket to the American flag. Ask not of what your pockets can do for you, but what you can do for your pockets.

Hidden Pockets

These are my go-to pockets because they're just so stinking easy to install.

Pattern

You'll need four pocket pieces cut out in the awkward-af shape shown. The straight edge needs to be big enough for your hand; try making them the length from your out-stretched thumb to your pinky finger. I set my phone on the fabric when I draw out the shape to make sure it will fit with plenty of wiggle-room.

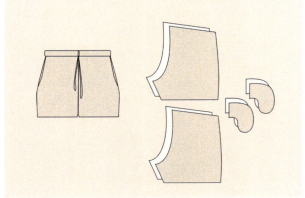

Step 1
Before any other sewing, all four pockets will be attached to the garment pieces. If you're using a circle-skirt pattern with one nice, continuous piece, you'll need to cut side seams through the whole piece to add pockets - don't try 'just cutting a small slit and attaching the pocket', it will look fucking dumb.

Step 2
When you sew the side seams shut, you'll follow this path instead; sew down to and around the pocket, pivoting at the pocket intersections. You'll want to iron the side seam flat near the pocket area or it looks like a vagina.

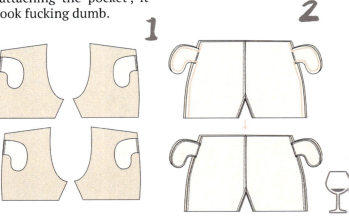

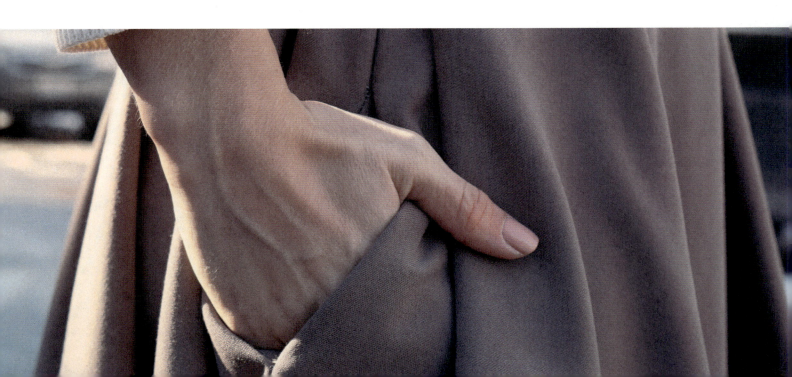

Sewn-to-Base

Of course you can just cut a pocket piece, slap it on the front of a garment with some top-stitching, and call it a day. This method makes the same type of pocket, but hides the bulk of the extra pocket fabric on the inside.

Pattern

On the front pattern piece, cut an indent out of the side top corner where the pocket's front edge will be (straight, curved, whatever).

The pocket piece will need to 'finish' the top corner of the garment, and then extend down the side and into the waistline.

Step 1
Attach these pockets before any other sewing is done. If your fabric is going to fray, finish the cut edge of the front piece and the inside edge of the pocket piece.

Step 2
Fold over the front piece edge and topstitch in place.

Step 3
Lay the pocket face-down on the *wrong side* of the main fabric and pin it down. Sewing from either the front or back, stitch along the pocket edge. Optionally attach the side and top to keep it in place.

Step 4
Use the pattern piece as normal, pretending the pocket is just a part of the front piece. The side of the pocket will be secured in side seam, and the top of the pocket will be secured in the waistband seam.

Peek-a-Boo

The previous pocket's sneaky friend, get the same peak-a-boo effect without visible stitching on the main fabric.

Pattern

On the front pattern piece, cut an indent out of the top corner (straight, curved, whatever).

One pocket piece will be cut with the same cut-out top corner as the pattern piece. The second pocket piece will need to 'finish' the top corner of the garment.

Step 1
Right sides together, make a seam along the inside corner of the pocket pieces.

Step 2
Flip the pocket right-side-out - that step is fucking important. Right sides together, connect the cut edge of the pocket to the cut edge of the main fabric.

Step 3
Flip the pocket back right-side in so the back panel 'peaks out' behind the main fabric. Make a small stitch-line on the top and side of the pocket to keep it in place, and then use the pattern piece as if the pocket and main fabric are just one piece.

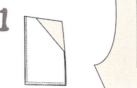

T-Shirt Pockets

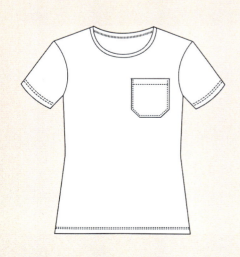

Regular t-shirt-esque pockets are super duper easy (find sweatshirt pockets in the directions for sweatshirts on page 49). Pocket, lock-it, and drop-it.

Pattern

The typical t-shirt pocket shape, a little wider and longer than you want the final pocket to be so the top can be folded over and the edges can be tucked under.

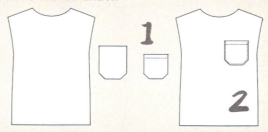

Step 1
It's easiest to attach the pocket before the front and back pieces are connected, but you may need to wait until the whole shebang is sewn to know exactly where you want the pocket to go.

Step 2
Fold over the top edge and topstitch in place. Tuck the edges of the pocket under and pin in place. Topstitch that mother-may-I down and you are done.

Zippers

The devil works hard, but zippers work harder. Zippers are essential for anything fitted, but it might take you a few wrong turns of installing it backwards, inside out, and misaligned before you make it out on the other side. If you're going through hell, keep on sewing.

Tip: Your zipper foot will always be attached on the side closest to the zipper.

Parts of a Zipper

Top Stops stop the slider at the top from running off the teeth.
Teeth are the bits that lock together and come apart when you zip.
Slider is the thing you pull on to zip and unzip, tab and all.
Bottom Stop(s) keeps the slider at the bottom. Separating zippers come apart at the bottom - one side traps the slider from falling off, and the other slips into and out of the slider.
Tape is the fabric strip holding the teeth that is sewn to the garment.

Shortening Zippers

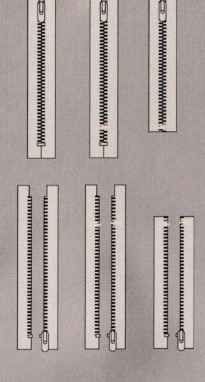

Regular Zipper
Shortening a regular, connected zipped will happen at the bottom stop of the zipper. Before installing the zipper, pin the zipper in place and mark the new bottom stop on the zipper itself. Unpin the zipper and, keeping it closed, make several stitches across both rows of teeth, creating a new bottom stop. This can be done with a machine, but is much faster to just do by hand. You can cut the rest of the zipper off below the new bottom stop if it's dangling in the way.

Separating Zipper
If a zipper completely separates when opened, you have to shorten that shit at the top, as to not fuck with the delicate engineering of the bottom stops. Before installing, while the zipper is zipped up, pin the zipper in place and mark the new top stops on both sides of the zipper. Then, unpin and unzip completely. Make several over-edge stitches across the top teeth on each side, creating new top stops. Some machines don't include an over-edge stitch, but this is much more easily done by hand, anyhow. You can cut the rest of the zipper off about half an inch above the top stops

Regular Zipper

By 'regular zipper', I mean any ol' regular zipper you see out in the wild – the teeth of the zipper are more or less visible when zipped up. For first-timers to the zipper foot, practice with a zipper, a piece of scrap fabric, and an un-threaded top needle.

Step 1
Finish the edges of the fabric at the zipper seam – skip this step if you're using a knit fabric that doesn't need edge finishing.

Step 2
With the right sides of the fabric together, make a full seam at least a half an inch wide – any smaller and it will be a pain in the ass to catch the seam allowance.

Step 3
Press the seam allowance flat and pin the zipper, completely zipped-up, face-down right at the seam line. These next few steps are illustrated upside-down because it makes more sense when you're at the machine.

Step 4
Put a pin through the fabric just above the bottom stop so you can see it from the other side. If you've got a zipper foot, pop it into your machine.

Step 5
From the top side of the fabric, you'll stitch across the bottom from right to left, pivot, and then up the left side of the zipper. Let's break this down: your bottom stitches should be below your pin marker and you will sew directly into/over your zipper. The zipper foot helps keep the side stitch line outside of the teeth. Tip - the zipper foot will always be attached on the side closest to the zipper. ✔

Step 6
Switch your zipper foot to the other side. This time, you'll stitch across the bottom from left to right, pivot, and then stitch up the right side.

Step 7
Use a seam ripper to remove the seam stitches hiding the zipper up to the bottom-stop. Zippity-do-fuck-yeah.

   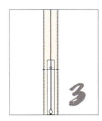 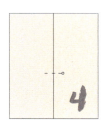   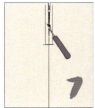

Separating Zipper

For separating zippers, you can follow the regular zipper steps and skip the bottom-stop stitch lines, or use this technique for bulkier projects.

Step 1
Optionally finish the cut edge. Fold the seam allowance under and pin the zipper sides in place, with teeth right along the folds.

Step 2
Top-stitch the zipper in place on each side. Once both sides are secured, zip to check how the fabric edges match up – you might have to redo one or both sides to get both sides aligned properly.

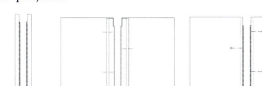

Regular Zipper with Lining

Step 1
Finish the cut edges on the main fabric and lining fabric, and make a seam at least a half an inch inward on both.

Step 2
If your lining is already connected to the main fabric, at the collar for example, flip the main fabric up and out of the way. On the lining, press the seam allowance flat and pin the zipper face-up along the seam line. Attach the zipper to the lining fabric following the same instructions as a regular zipper (above): stitch across the bottom and up the right, then across the bottom and up the left.

Step 3
If your main fabric and lining are connected, fold the main fabric back down, right-side out. Pin the main fabric, zipper tape, and lining together, with the seams aligned. Top-stitch on the main fabric, the same way you would attach a regular zipper – you'll be sewing through the main fabric, zipper tape, and lining fabric. When finished, the lining will show double rows of stitches around the zipper.

Step 4
Use the seam ripper to open the zipper down to the bottom stop stitches on both the main fabric and lining fabric.

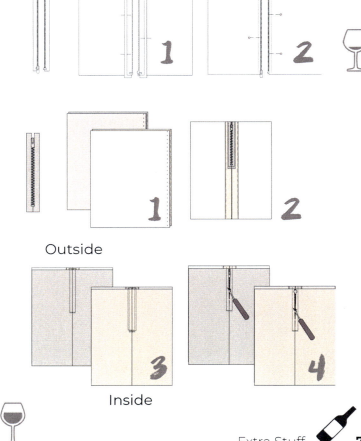

Outside

Inside

Invisible Zipper

Stores sell special invisible zippers that are meant to be hidden when installed – you'll know it's an invisible zipper by the word 'invisible' on the packaging, fucking duh. You want as little a gap as possible between the fabrics at the seam, so putting that sneaky sucker in is a little different.

Step 1
Finish the edges of the fabric at the zipper seam – skip this for knit fabrics that don't need edge finishing when you're feeling lazy.

Step 2
This is where things gets weird. Unzipped, pin the right-hand zipper side face-down to the nice side of the fabric, as shown (See? Confusing to explain in words). Make a stitch line all the way down to the slider.

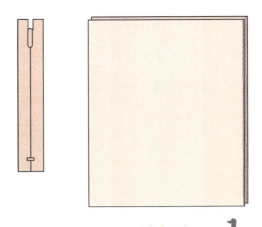

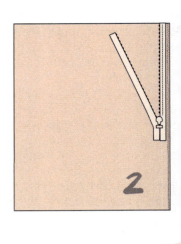

Invisible Zipper with Lining

There are two methods to inserting an invisible zipper into a garment with lining, equally challenging but practical for different situations.

> **Method #1**

Good for tops and dresses, where the collar is connected before your zipper is inserted, or skirts that won't have an attached waistband. Works well with lighter, easy-to-use fabrics.

Step 1
Complete the main fabric and lining, leaving one seam open for the zipper on both. Finish the seam edges if the fabric will unravel. ✗

Step 2
If you're working with a top or dress, your garment will already be attached at the collar. Else wise, pin the lining to the main fabric, right-sides together, and make a continuous seam along the top.

Step 3
Flip the lining fabric up and out of the way. Attach the right side of the invisible zipper to the main fabric as shown (look to the invisible zipper instructions on the previous page for details).

Step 4
Attach the left side of the invisible zipper, again referring to the invisible zipper instructions for more detail. This will take some finagling, and will look similar to this when done.

Step 5
Flip the lining fabric down so it is inside out, and pin in place. This will seem completely incorrect, but make a line of stitches in the seam allowance, between the teeth and the cut edge. You'll be sewing through the lining, zipper tape, and main fabric, and sew as far down to the bottom stop as possible.

Step 6
Flip the main fabric inside-out, and pull the lining and main fabric apart like so. Finish the seam by stitching from the join to the hem on both parts.

72

Fly-Front Not Fucking Covered

Some garments, like jeans, have a lapped or fly-front seam, where a little flap hides the zipper. That shit is not covered in this guide, but the internet can get you where you need to be.

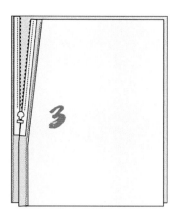

Step 3

Figuring out how to pin the left zipper side to the fabric is the big goddamn mystery. It will need to be pinned to the nice side of the fabric, but requires some flipping around to a manageable position as shown. Once you've solved the puzzle, make another stitch line down to the slider.

Pause, turn the garment right-side-out, zip up, and evaluate. You'll end up re-doing invisible zippers about half the time because it's backwards, twisted, or some other fresh hell.

Step 4

To finish the seam, pin the fabric right-sides together and pull the zipper bottom out of the way. Start the seam as close to the zipper stitches as possible, overlapping about an inch, and stitch down the rest of the seam line.

Method #2

Good for skirts and bottoms where a waistband will be added after the zipper is installed. Works better for thicker materials.

Step 1

Complete the main fabric and lining, leaving one seam open for the zipper on both. Optionally finish the seam edges.

Step 2

Attach the right side of the invisible zipper to the main fabric as shown (refer to the invisible zipper instructions for more detail).

Step 3

Attach the left side of the invisible zipper, referring to the invisible zipper instructions on above for more detail. This will take some finagling, and will look similar to the illustration when finished.

Step 4

Pin the lining to the main fabric, right sides together. In the seam allowance, between the teeth and the cut edge, stitch through the lining, zipper, tape, and main fabric. The stitching will go as close to the bottom stop as possible.

Step 5

If you're adding a waistband, you can skip this step. If you need the waist closed, make a line of continuous stitches along the top.

Step 6

Flip the main fabric inside-out, and pull the lining and main fabric apart like so. Finish the seam by stitching from the join to the hem on both parts.

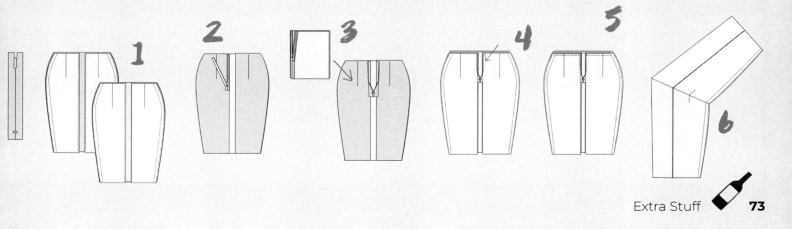

Buttons

They may seem daunting, but(ton) don't worry – most machines nowadays come with an incredibly easy-to-use buttonhole setting and/or foot to make buttons a breeze. When adding buttons to a spot under a lot of strain (waistbands, between your shoulder blades, or that one poor button right between your tits), consider using interfacing (page 86) to reinforce that sucker. With a little practice, they can be a button(w)hole lot more simple than expected.

Making a Buttonhole

Practice

Practice making your button-hole with the button you've picked, the exact same fabric, and the same number of fabric layers you'll actually use. You don't want to make four beautiful buttonholes in your garment and realize they're not big enough.

Measure

For multiple buttons, measure the distance from the first button placement to the last button placement, and then divide that by one less than the number of buttons you're using. Math.

Mark

If you're hand-making your buttonholes, mark both ends of your evenly-spaced button-holes with pins or pencil. For machine-made buttonholes, heck it and just mark one end.

Make

Buttonhole Foot

Do a little dance if your machine has a built-in buttonhole stitch and/or buttonhole foot attachment. A buttonhole foot is a handy little fella that your button clips into, and the size of the buttonhole is magically perfect. Check your machine manual for the exact ins and outs of buttonhole feet.

 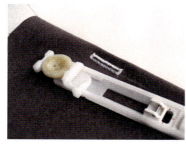

Both machine-made and hand-made buttonholes follow the same-ish steps, using a very skinny zig-zag stitch.

What makes a good buttonhole?

✔ Big enough to slide the button through, but not slip out

✔ The thicker the fabric, the bigger the button and buttonhole

✘ None of the stitches were cut open when making the slit

✘ Buttons will not poke over the garment edges or other seams when slipped through the buttonholes

✔ Those sonsofbitches are all straight and in line

✔ They are evenly spaced out

✔ Horizontal buttonholes are stronger and more secure, but vertical buttonholes are common for tops and small buttons

Disclaimer: These stitches look shitty because hand-made buttonholes are hard as fuck. Pray for a buttonhole foot.

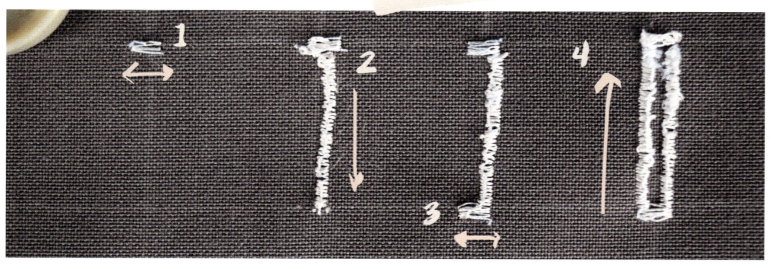

Step 1
At one end 4 or 5 wide stitches are made all the way across the buttonhole – this is considered the 'bar tack' that keeps your hole secure.

Step 2
Switch to a shallower zig-zag stitch to sew down one side of the buttonhole.

Step 3
The second bar tack is made with 4 or 5 wide stitches.

Step 4
Either the machine magically changes direction or you pivot the fabric to sew up the other side of the buttonhole with more shallow stitches.

Opening a Buttonhole

Step 1
Put pins in each end of the buttonhole to prevent cutting through the bar tack stitches.

Step 2
Put your seam ripper or scissors into the center of the buttonhole and carefully snip it open. If you accidentally slice a few stitches, some glue will tack it in place.

 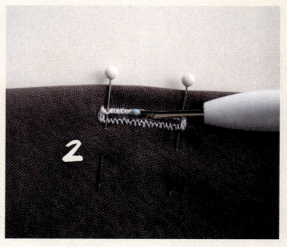

Attaching a Button

Step 1
Line your fabric up exactly where you want the buttons and holes to align. Put a pin in the center of the buttonholes.

Step 2
Slide your buttonholes up and over the pins, and then mark the center spot.

Step 3
Pull a threaded needle through right at the center spot. Keep your thread doubled-up for a stronger, lazier attachment.

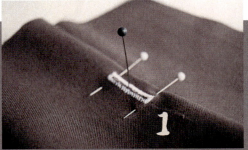

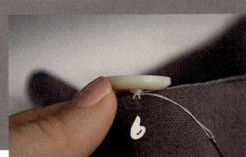

Step 4
Bring the needle up through one hole of the button, and then down through a different hole of the button and through the fabric. Leave some wiggle-room for your button to lift away from the fabric a teensy bit and have space for the buttonhole fabric.

Step 5
Crisscross or parallel, it doesn't matter, but be consistent. Repeat until you feel confident in that sonofabitch.

Step 6
Wrap your thread around the under-stitches a few times and then knot in place. Cut your threads close enough to be hidden by the button.

After attaching a button, you might want to fasten it into its buttonhole and check the placement of the next button to make sure shit will lie flat in-between.

Button Foot
Some machines also have a superbly helpful button foot, but you're limited by how thick or wide of a button it can handle. Sneak a peak at your manual for button foot instructions.

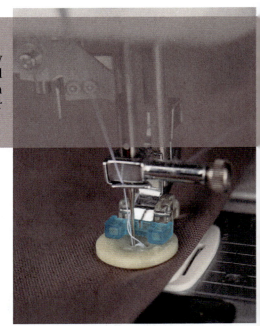

Hooks and Eyes

Hooks and eyes are a good alternative to buttons when you need something less conspicuous or you're just too damn lazy to install a friggin' buttonhole.

Regular hooks and eyes are found where fabrics meet but don't overlap, like necklines or above a zipper. Heavy-duty hooks and eyes are used for thicker fabrics, spots under a lot of strained like waistbands, and areas where the fabric overlaps and needs to be closed.

Hook

Eye

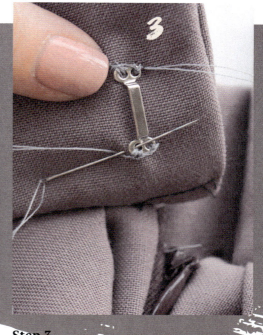

Step 1
Attach a heavy-duty hook on the inside of the flap - there's no special way to do this, just tack that shit in place with a few hand-made stitches. If you want the hook to be well-hidden, make sure to only stitch into the underside fabric layer, not through to the outer fabric.

Step 2
Pin the eye opposite the hook, gauging the alignment as best as you can.

Step 3
Use a few more hand-made stitches to secure the eye in place – make these stitches through to all layers of fabric for added reinforcement, as they'll be hidden inside the waistband.

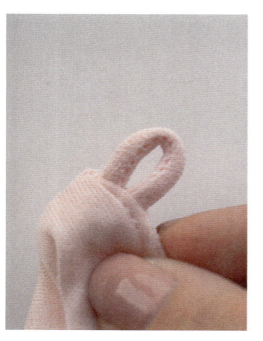

Fabric Eyes
Fabric eyes are used with decorative buttons, or just for the hell of it. If you're slipping a fabric eye over a button, be sure your fabric is a little stretchy, or use elastic. Make a very small strap using the stitch-and-turn technique from page 66, large enough to stretch over the button. To gauge the right size loop, pinch the two ends of the mini strap together and try to slip or stretch the loop over the button. Either sew the eye to the underside of the garment or sandwich the loop in between the lining and main fabric.

Regular

Heavy Duty

Elastic

Elastic is a true ally to lazy people - it's the symbolic shoulder-shrug of the sewing world. What exact size should these pants be? Elastic. How do I avoid installing a zipper? Elastic. When adding elastic, fabric openings (waistbands, wrists, ankles, etc) should be big enough to easily slip on, and elastic pieces should hug the spot comfortably. There are a few methods for adding elastic that you'll find useful for different projects; all good, all easy, all here to make your life more snug.

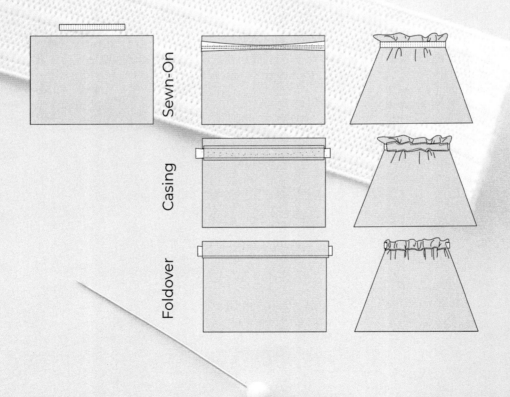

Sewn-On

Casing

Foldover

Sewn-On

Elastic can be sewn directly to your fabric, either on the inside or used as a circular waistband (page 67). Sewn-on is perfect if you don't mind the elastic being visible from the inside.

Step 1
On your fabric and elastic separately, mark the middle and side points.

Step 2
Pin the elastic to the fabric, matching up the marks. Pin the elastic in more places if it's being particularly fussy.

Step 3
Sew through both the elastic and fabric with a straight or zig-zag stitch. While sewing, gently stretch the elastic between the pins - don't yank the damned fabric through your machine, just guide it along.

Step 4
If you are using wider elastic, you might make two or three rows of stitches.

Casing/Sheath

If you want your elastic hidden on the inside, make an elastic casing and pull your elastic through.

Step 1
Cut a piece of fabric wider than your elastic and pin to the wrong side of the fabric. Fold the edges under if you're feeling particularly thorough (I wasn't).

Step 2
Make a straight stitch along the top of the casing and another along the bottom.

Step 3
Pull the elastic through the casing. Helpful hint: using a safety pin makes it much easier to thread the elastic through.

Step 4
Overlap the elastic ends and stitch them together. You'll need to tug the elastic up and away from the fabric to do this, which can be awkward-as-hell to maneuver.

Foldover

Adding elastic into a fold-over waistband is so fucking easy.

Step 1
With your garment inside-out, fold your waistband over far enough to fit your elastic. Make a straight stitch line at the bottom of the waistband - leaving a small gap to thread in your elastic.

Step 2
Pull the elastic through the waistband. Use your bestie, the safety pin.

Step 4
Overlap the elastic ends and stitch them together. You'll need to tug the elastic ends up and away from the fabric to do this.

Step 5
Stretch your fabric to pull the elastic fully into the waistband and stitch the gap closed.

Gathers

Gathers happen when a piece of fabric is scrunched up and attached to a shorter, flat length of fabric (for gathers made by elastic, skip to page 78). As a basic rule of thumb, the longer the gather-side fabric, the more scrunched your gathered fabric looks. I wouldn't suggest making your gather fabric more than three times the length of your straight-side fabric, but there's no right or wrong fabric length to choose. You'll learn to gauge that sort of stuff accordingly.

Machines sometimes have a gather foot or special gather feeds - refer to your manual for that fun shit. I'm going to outline the two laziest ways to add gathers in your life.

Lazy

Step 1
Loosen your upper thread tension and make one long machine-baste stitch line or hand-baste stitch line (page 16) all along the edge where you want the gathers, careful not to back-stitch at either end, because you'll be pulling this thread out eventually. Some people make a second baste stitch line parallel to the first but that's one more whole stupid step.

Step 2
Slide your fabric along the stitch line to make small, even-ish gathers until the scrunched fabric is the right length. Knot the ends of the stitches to keep the gathers from slipping.

Step 3
Pin your gathered fabric evenly to your flat fabric. When you feed your fabric through the machine, sew with the gathered fabric on top when. Make a straight stitch across the gathers, and snip any baste stitch threads visible from the right side.

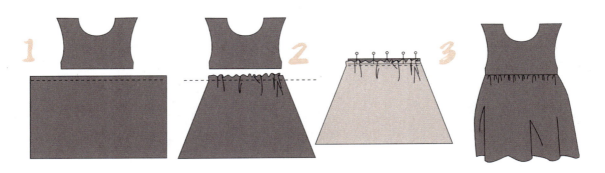

Laziest

Step 1
Pin your gather fabric directly onto your flat fabric, trying to make the gaps as even as possible. This method inevitably ends as a messy mix between gathers and pleats and that's just fine by my standards.

Step 2
Sew with the gathered fabric on top when feeding your piece through the machine. You may end up tucking folds under the foot or holding the gathers in place with your left hand while you push the fabric through.

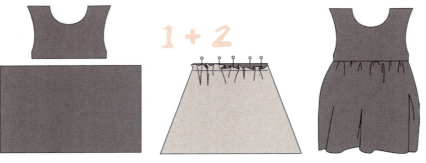

Pleats

Pleats are the sophisticated older sibling of gathers – folds of fabric are spaced out evenly and deliberately, giving a cleaner look. Like gathers, adding pleats requires extra fabric length, and more damned math. Pleats are an excellent option for thicker fabrics that are too stiff for gathers.

There are one-fold pleats and two-fold pleats. One-fold pleats, called side or knife pleats, are single folds (usually) all turned in the same direction. Two-fold, or double-fold, pleats are made when two folds are made either away from each other (box pleats), or towards each other (inverted peats).

How many pleats to add, where to put them, and how deep the folds are is entirely up to you. A good place to start would be three to four single-pleats per front and back, or two to three two-fold pleats per front and back.

Add the extra pleat fabric number just where the pleats will be placed. If the pleats will all be at the skirt waist, you would add the extra pleat fabric just to your skirt waist measurement, not to the hem or anywhere-the-hell else.

Decide how many pleats you'll be doing and how many inches deep a pleat will be, then multiply by two (since a fold goes in and then back out again).

E.G. If you're doing four one-fold pleats on the front, and four one-fold pleats on the back that are one inch deep, you'll add

(8 total pleats x 1 inch x 2) = 16 inches

If you're doing three two-fold pleats on the front and three two-fold pleats on the back that are 1 inch deep, you'll add

(6 total pleats x 2 folds each x 1 inch x 2) = 24 inches

Making Pleats

There are ways to make more precise, perfectly-positioned pleats, but here's the barely-enough-fucks-to-give method.

Note: Inverted pleats look shitty when they end up with a big gap between them. To sidestep this problem, either baste stitch farther into the fabric, lower than where your seam will be made, or add extra pins to keep the pleat closed when sewing.

Step 1
Make a mark for each pleat, evenly-spaced.

Step 2
Fold the fabric at each point - fold to one side of the mark for single pleats, and on both sides for double pleats.

Step 3
As added security, baste stitch the pleats in place, ripping out any visible baste stitches when the garment is finished.

One-Fold

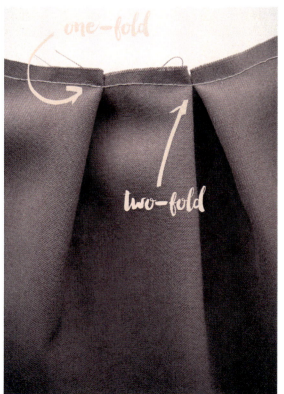

Two-Fold

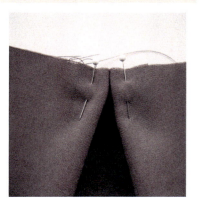

Darts

Save the curves of your tits and ass by learning the what, why, where and how of making darts in the most lackadaisical way possible.

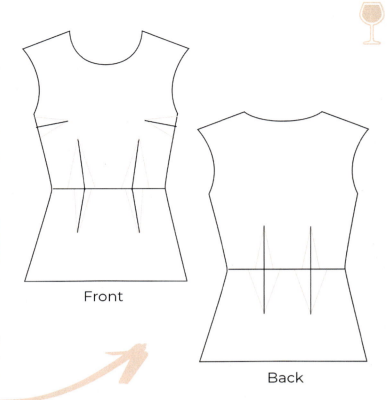

Front

Back

What the fuck is a dart?

A dart is a cut into a garment that gives some curve to the flat piece of fabric, making it fit better around your boobs and bum. There are single-pointed darts that look like a triangle, and double-pointed darts shaped like a diamond.

Why the fuck do we need darts?

Without darts, fitted tops squash your tits down

and pencil skirts smash your ass into an ugly square. Even loose clothing, like t-shirts, sometimes use darts for a nicer shape.

Where the fuck do darts go?

Single-pointed darts are most commonly found to the side of your boob, directly underneath your boob, or right above your rear end. Double-pointed darts are used at the waistline to make sheath dresses fit like a glove.

How the fuck to add darts:

Measuring for Darts

Tits: There are all sorts of meticulous measurements you can make around your chest - but only two numbers are needed to make passable darts; your bust size, measured over the fullest part of your boobs, and your high bust, measured from right under your armpits.

If you're curious about what other useful measurements to take, make note of how far south your nip is from your shoulder, the length from the side seam to your nipple, how far apart your tatas are, and how close your tits are to your waistline.

Ass: For basic booty-poppin' darts, measure your waistline where the garment will hit, and the fullest part of your hips.

Adding Darts to a Pattern

On a top, the base of the dart triangles will be your full bust measurement minus your high bust measurement, divided by two. If your full bust is 35" and high bust is 32", your dart widths will be 1.5" (35"-32" / 2). Generally (don't fucking quote me),

A-cup: 1/2" darts	C-cup: 1.5" darts
B-cup: 1" darts	D-cup: 2" darts

The darts should 'point' roughly at your nip, but stop ¾"-1" short. Whether you measure, mark, or eyeball this spot, you'll end up making a few too-low and too-high darts. The good news is even an 'off' dart is better than a flattened uni-boob.

If you're making side darts, add length to your front pattern piece so that, once the darts are made, the side seams of the front and back pattern pieces are equal. If you've opted for under-boob darts, add width to just the bottom hem of your front pattern piece. It's hard to explain but you'll figure it out.

For skirts, the base of the dart triangles will be super-duper-roughly your hip measurement minus your waist measurement, divided by the number of darts, divided by 2. For example, if your hips are 40" and your waist is 30", and you're using just two darts, your dart triangles will be

(40" hips - 30" waist) / (2 darts x 2) = 2.5" wide

There are more precise ways to do this, but we are here for a good time, not a long time.

The darts should 'point' right at the fullest part of your caboose, and stop ¾"-1" short of your hipline.

Single Darts

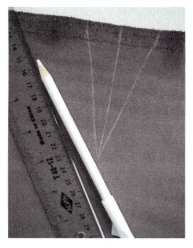   

Step 1
Mark your darts on the wrong side of the fabric. Mark mirrored darts at the same time to so they're symmetrical.

Step 2
Fold the dart down the center, lining up the dart slopes, and pin in place.

Step 3
Starting from the outer edge of the dart, make a straight stitch along the dart slope all the way to the point - it's alright to sew off the edge of the fabric. You can backstitch at the beginning and the end of the dart, but any backstitching at the point should be inside the dart fabric.

Step 4
For most fabrics, just press the excess dart fabric to one side and catch it in the side seam to hold it in place.

With thicker fabrics, slit the dart down the center and press flat.

Diamond Darts

 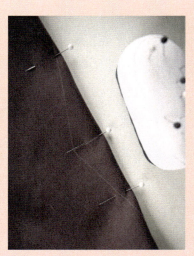 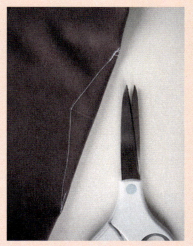 

Step 1
Mark your darts on the wrong side of the fabric. Mark mirrored darts at the same time so they're symmetrical.

Step 2
Fold the dart down the center line and pin in place.

Step 3
Start at the widest part of the dart and make a straight stitch along one dart slope to the point - it's alright to sew off the edge of the fabric. Backstitch at the point inside the dart. Repeat with the second side of the dart.

Step 4
To help a diamond dart lay flat, make a few snips into the excess dart fabric.

Lining

Lining is useful for three things: hiding ugly seams, protecting your delicate skin from a scratchy main fabric, and making see-through fabric less 'Rihanna' and more 'family reunion'. Lining is annoying as hell (you're basically making a second garment and then some) but pays off in the end, so get to work work work work work work.

Choosing Lining Fabric

First and foremost, make sure to pick a lining with the same stretchiness as the outer fabric. I've made this mistake and you, too, will end up sausage-stuffed into a lining with no give while your beautiful outer-garment was made with perfect stretch. Hold a layer of lining to your main fabric and stretch the two together to see if they're ~simpatico~.

The lining color doesn't matter unless your main fabric is lace or sheer, or if the lining peeps out from under the skirt. Contrasting or matching, it doesn't matter.

Normally, the lining you choose will be of lighter weight than your main fabric; light-weight cottons, silks, and rayon are great because they're breathable, static-free, and durable. Pro-tip, some excellent light knits are hidden in the dance and cosplay sections.

Lining Skirts Without Zippers

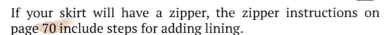

If your skirt will have a zipper, the zipper instructions on page 70 include steps for adding lining.

Step 1
Cut your skirt pattern out from the lining fabric. The skirt lining can be a few inches shorter than your main skirt hem.

Step 2
Sew up the main skirt and lining skirt separately, except for the hem and waistline. If your skirt will have pockets, add them to the main fabric skirt and ignore them in your lining skirt.

Step 3
Pin the main fabric to the lining fabric at the waist, wrong-sides together. This will make sure the seam finishes on both the main fabric and lining are hidden in-between. Optionally baste stitch the lining in place right at the waist line.

Step 4
Attach the waistband (page 66) to both the main fabric and the lining fabric. When you sew, you'll be stitching through the waistband fabric, the main fabric, and the lining fabric.

Step 5
Hem the main fabric and lining fabric separately, turning the hem on both 'inward' where the seams are.

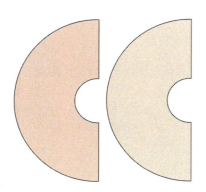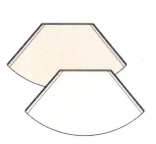

Lining Tops and One-Piece Dresses

Adding lining to a two-piece dress can be found on page 60.

Step 1
It's not the worst idea to wash your main fabric and lining fabric before sewing. Separately, shrinkage is annoying but harmless. If that shit shrinks while attached, you're fucked.

From your lining fabric, cut a second pair of front and back pieces. In these instructions, we won't line the sleeves, so don't bother cutting out extra sleeve pieces.

If you're making darts, add them to the front pieces of both the main and lining fabric. This step is way easier to do before anything is attached.

Step 2
Sewing with right sides together, connect the main fabric and lining fabric at the shoulders.

Step 3
Lining fabric is usually connected to the main fabric at the collar the same way that facing is connected (page 65). Pin your lining fabric to your main fabric around the collar, with the right-sides of the fabrics together. When the lining is flipped inward, the seam finishes of both the lining and the main fabric will be hidden in-between.

Without Zipper

With Zipper

Step 4
Flip the lining inside the garment and finish the collar with an understitch or topstitch. Again, the facing instructions on page 65 go into more detail about collar finishes.

Step 5
Pull the lining out of the way, and pin the right-sides of the main fabric together at the side seams. Sew the side seams up, stopping at the arm hole.

Step 6
Now, pull the main fabric out of the way and pin the right-sides of the lining fabric together at the side seams. Sew the side seams up, stopping at the armhole. When the main fabric is pulled back down again, the seam-finishes of both the main fabric and lining fabric will be hidden, 'sandwiched' in the middle.

Step 7
For sleeveless tops, the easy finish is to fold over the armhole cut edges and top-stitch in place. If you want the armhole stitching to be hidden, get your ass over to Google, because this guide does not cover that complicated mess.

If you're adding sleeves, baste-stitch your lining fabric to your main fabric at the armhole. When you attach the sleeves, you'll sew through the sleeve fabric, the main bodice fabric, and the lining fabric.

For dresses with zippers, follow the zipper instructions from page 70.

When Hemming:
You can hem the lining and main fabric separately, or 'catch' the lining fabric in the main fabric hem.

Fucking Interfacing

What in the ever-living fuck is interfacing? Well, it's basically a thicker or stiffer layer of fabric on the inside of a garment that helps gives shape and support. If you're working with very flimsy fabric, sewing interfacing into places like buttonhole strips, waistbands, and cuffs adds extra stability and thickness to the fabric. As a newbie to the sewing game, you probably won't seek out structural interfacing unless a pattern mentions it, but it's still a good thing to keep in the back of your mind.

As a member of Team Lazy, one type of interfacing you might find bonkers useful is called fusible web. Fusible web is a special, sticky strip of interfacing that binds two layers of fabric together when ironed into place - perfect for no-sew hems or attaching appliqués.

Types of Interfacing

Texture

Woven Woven interfacing has a visible grain, which means it needs to be cut along the same grainline as the garment. Woven interfacing usually has no give, so it shouldn't be used with stretchy material. Heckin' waste of time.

Non-Woven Non-woven interfacings have no grainline, and therefore can be cut in any direction. With little give, non-woven interfacing is a great option for most beginner projects that don't use stretchy fabrics.

Knit Knit interfacing does have some stretch, but only in one direction. You'll need to be careful what direction you're cutting the interfacing pattern so that the stretchy direction is compatible with your garment.

Thickness

Interfacing comes in a shit-ton of different 'weights'. FAPFSs say to choose a weight equal to or lighter than your fabric, but since I don't know what the fuck that means, just feel out the thickness and stiffness of the options and go with your heart.

Application

Sew-In Sew-in interfacing is held in place by the seams and stitching along the main fabric. It takes more time and isn't as sturdy, so basically why fucking bother? The only reason you would choose this stupid option is for textured or delicate fabrics that can't handle fusible interfacing.

Fusible Fusible interfacing has a sticky coating on one side that melds to the wrong side of the fabric when ironed on. It's quick and easy, and is the obvious choice for most interfacing needs. Fabrics that can't handle the heat of fusing interfacing include super delicate fabrics, textured fabrics, and some knits, so practice with a teeny piece of interfacing and scrap fabric before going to town.

Waistband, etc There are some helpful, pre-cut interfacing pieces like waistbanding that keep you from buying, measuring, and cutting unnecessary amounts of regular interfacing.

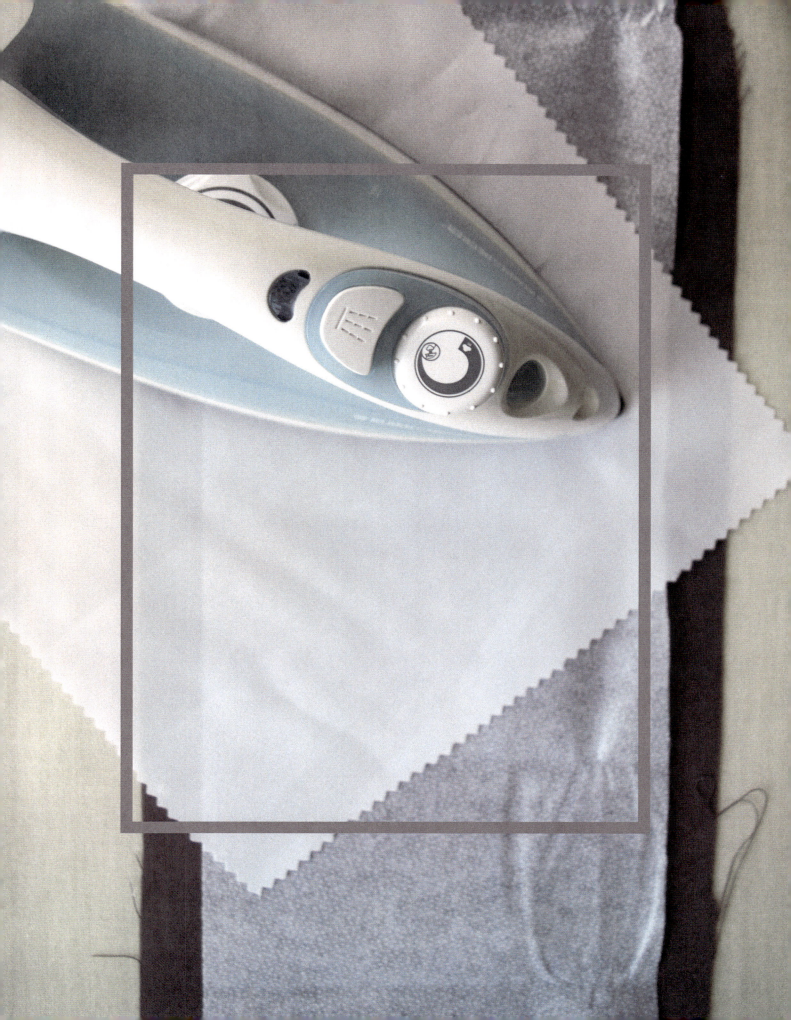

Alteration Station

French vanilla coffee creamer, boob jobs, and goat yoga - all proof that great things can be made even greater with just a little adjustment. Whether you're altering something off the shelf, hand-made, or hand-me-down'ed, here are some of the easiest tweaks to go from great to greater, still.

Shorten Shoulder

To shorten the shoulder of a top or dress, you have to first remove the sleeve (annoying but worth it). Use your seam ripper to free the sleeve seam, cut into the armhole, and then re-attach your sleeve (page 46).

Take In Sleeve

Over-sized sleeves are a super fucking simple fix. Turn your garment inside out and, starting from the armpit, straight-stitch down the length of the arm.

Shorten Sleeve

Cut the sleeve slightly longer than the sleeve length you have in mind. Turn your sleeve under at the right sleeve length and top-stitch in place.

Add Darts

Adding darts to a top is a great way to give shape and a little fit to a top. Use your seam ripper to open the side seams of the top, and install darts (page 82). Because the darts shorten the front pattern piece, you'll need to cut a few inches off of the back hem, sew the side seams back up, and finish the hem.

Take In Sides

Turn your garment inside-out and use a straight stitch to take in the sides of a top. Stitch just to the armpit, or keep sewing down the length of the sleeve for a total take-in. Sew straight down, or add a slight taper into the waistline for a more feminine fit.

Hem

Optionally seam-rip the original hem open, and cut excess fabric length off. Follow any hem suggestions from page 26 for a shorter hem.

Take In Waist From Behind

There are more complicated ways to take in the waist of a pair of pants, but the lazy way? Make a dart right at the back seam: fold the back seam together and sew a tapered straight-stitch down from the waist. If the waist needs to be taken in by more than two inches, consider also taking in the waist from the sides. Optionally re-attach any belt loops that might have been closed over.

Take In Waist From Side

Side darts can also be made to take in a waistline. With the pants flipped inside-out, sew a tapered straight-stitch down from the waist. If you see any noticeable puckering from the right-side of the fabric, you may need to make the dart longer for a more shallow taper. Optionally re-attache any belt loops that might have been closed over.

Take In From Side

Turn your pants inside-out and use a straight stitch all the way down to take in your pants from the side seams.

Take In From Inseam

Pants can also be taken in from the inseam, instead of the side seams. Turn your pants inside-out and use a straight stitch to sew up one inseam and back down the other.

Hem

Optionally seam-rip the original hem open, and cut excess fabric length off. Follow any hem suggestions from page 26 for a shorter hem.

Fabric Purchasing Guide

MISSES SIZES							
	0	**2**	**4**	**6**	**8**	**10**	**12**
	XS	XS	S	S	M	M	L
Bust	32+	33	34	35	36	37	38½
Waist	24½	25½	26½	27½	28½	30	31½
Hips	34½	35½	36½	37½	38½	39½	41
YDS OF FABRIC							
Tank Top	3/4	3/4	3/4	3/4	1	1	1
Tee Shirt	1 5/8	1 5/8	1 5/8	1 5/8	1 5/8	1 5/8	1 3/4
Long Sleeve Top	1 1/2	1 1/2	1 3/4	1 3/4	1 3/4	1 3/4	2
Hooded Sweatshirt	2 1/8	2 1/8	2 1/8	2 1/8	2 1/4	2 1/4	2 1/4
Pencil Skirt	1	1	1	1	1 1/8	1 1/8	1 1/8
Circle Skirt (Midi)	1 1/4	1 1/2	1 1/2	1 3/4	1 3/4	1 3/4	1 3/4
Maxi Skirt	1	1	1 1/4	1 1/4	1 1/2	1 1/2	1 1/2
Shorts	3/4	3/4	1	1	1 1/8	1 1/8	1 1/4
Pants	1 1/4	1 1/4	1 1/4	1 1/4	1 3/8	1 3/8	1 3/4
Shift dress							
Sleeveless	1 1/4	1 1/4	1 1/4	1 3/8	1 1/2	1 1/2	1 1/2
Short Sleeve	1 1/2	1 1/2	1 5/8	1 5/8	1 5/8	1 5/8	2 5/8
long sleeve	1 3/8	1 3/8	1 3/8	1 1/2	1 3/4	1 3/4	1 7/8
Sheath Dress							
sleeveless	1 1/4	1 3/8	1 3/8	1 1/2	1 5/8	1 5/8	1 3/4
short sleeve	1 1/2	1 1/2	1 1/2	1 5/8	1 3/4	1 3/4	1 7/8
long sleeve	1 5/8	1 5/8	1 5/8	1 7/8	1 7/8	1 7/8	2
A-Line Dress							
sleeveless	2	2	2	2 1/4	2 1/4	2 1/4	2 1/4
short sleeve	2 1/4	2 1/4	2 3/8	2 1/2	2 1/2	2 1/2	2 1/2
long sleeve	2 1/2	2 1/2	2 1/2	2 3/4	2 3/4	2 3/4	2 3/4
Maxi Dress							
spagetti strap	2 1/2	2 5/8	2 5/8	2 3/4	2 3/4	3	3
short sleeve	2 3/4	2 3/4	3	3 1/8	3 1/4	3 1/4	3 1/4
long sleeve	3	3	3 1/8	3 1/4	3 3/8	3 3/8	3 3/8

Measurements

Garment Type

If you choose a fabric with a 'right way' pattern, plaids, or napped fabrics like velvet, you'll need to buy ¼ yard extra for each yard needed, so all pieces can be cut facing the same direction.

Make note of how much fabric you buy for a project and adjust it when you're finished.

			Fabric Width 54-60"		
14	16	18	20	22	24
L	XL	XL	XXL	XXL	XXL
40	41½	43	44	45	46
33	34½	36	39	41	43
42½	44	45½	47	48	49
1	1 1/4	1 1/4	1 1/4	1 1/4	1 1/4
1 3/4	1 3/4	1 3/4	2	2	2
2	2 1/8	2 1/8	2 1/4	2 1/4	2 1/4
2 1/4	2 3/8	2 3/8	2 1/2	2 1/2	2 1/2
1 1/8	1 1/4	1 1/4	1 1/2	1 1/2	1 1/2
1 7/8	1 7/8	1 7/8	2	2	2
1 1/2	1 3/4	1 3/4	1 3/4	2	2
1 1/4	1 3/8	1 3/8	1 1/2	1 1/2	1 1/2
1 3/4	1 3/4	1 7/8	1 7/8	2	2
1 1/2	1 1/2	1 3/4	2	2 1/8	2 1/8
2 5/8	2 5/8	2 5/8	2 7/8	2 7/8	2 7/8
1 7/8	1 7/8	2	2	2 1/2	2 1/2
1 3/4	1 3/4	1 3/4	1 7/8	1 7/8	1 7/8
1 7/8	1 7/8	1 7/8	2	2	2
2	2	2	2 1/4	2 1/4	2 1/4
2 5/8	2 5/8	2 3/4	2 3/4	2 3/4	2 7/8
2 3/4	2 3/4	2 7/8	2 7/8	2 7/8	3
3 1/8	3 1/8	3 1/8	3 1/8	3 1/8	3 1/4
3 1/4	3 1/4	3 1/4	3 1/4	3 1/2	3 1/2
3 3/8	3 3/8	3 1/2	3 1/2	3 5/8	3 5/8
3 1/2	3 1/2	3 5/8	3 5/8	3 3/4	3 3/4

Shift Dress

Sheath Dress

A-Line Dress

Maxi Dress

*These are some fucking rooough estimates. Yardage can differ between patterns and how good you are at tetris-ing the pieces. Don't '@' me that you maybe had to make an extra trip to the store.

Special Thanks

Pour one out for every person along the road who's given me a tiny push forward,

let's sit down to a glass of wine some time and catch up.

Thank you to the teachers I've had that challenged me; **Susan Ruen**, who instilled in me a love of books, **Patty Ohl** for teaching me about creativity and page layouts way back when it was physically cutting out content, and **Justin Garvin,** who made me ask questions, find answers, and teach myself.

Endless heaps of gratitude to my family - your continual outpouring of support and praise has given me an absurdly large ego and even bigger dreams. Especially to **Rhonda Halfpop, Allison McKinney-Feldman, Morgan Dornbier,** and my parents, **Leslie Dornbier** and **Damon Dornbier**, thank you for teaching me how to curse and how to drink wine.

Thank you to my grandpa, **Ronald Pals**, and in loving memory of his wife, **Melva June** - you make us all get our shit together, everyday.

To every friend who's ever seen my ridiculous projects and told me, with a straight face, that they thought I was cool - you will never, ever, know how much that means to me. Thank you for tolerating my overwhelming enthusiasm for themed events and encouraging me to be over-the-top. Special shoutouts to **Sara Mulders, Brooke Davis,** and **Avery Stahr** for indulging my lunacy.

Cheers to you all.

Kaitlyn Dornbier is a Chicago-based software engineer, dog enthusiast, audiobook devotee, and overall crafter. She started her sewing journey by making a black birthday dress she couldn't find online, and has been stumbling along through projects ever since. Her work has been shown nowhere but her own Instagram and in her family group chat. She cannot emphasize enough how fucking little she knows what she's doing, but she's having a good time along the way.

www.kdornbier.com

Index

not your grandma's sewing guide

not your grandma's sewing guide

Made in the USA
Monee, IL
06 December 2022